# EASY PIANO LEARNING FOR KIDS

## Master Notes, Keys, and Rhythms with Fun and Simple Exercises

Clara Forte

Copyright © Clara Forte 2024. All Rights Reserved.

No part of this book may be reproduced, stored, distributed, or transmitted in any form or by any means, including photocopying, recording, or other electronic or mechanical methods, without the prior written permission of the copyright holder, except in the case of brief quotations embodied in critical reviews and certain other noncommercial uses permitted by copyright law.

# TABLE OF CONTENTS

Description      Page

## Introduction — 03

- Welcome to Your Musical Adventure
- Discover how this book combines fun activities and essential music notation to engage and educate young pianists. Designed for both parents and teachers, it makes learning enjoyable and effective.

## Learning Notes — 05

- Basics of Piano Symbols
- Hand Positions (Left and Right)
- Line and Space Notes
- Bass and Treble Clefs
- Note Names and Memorization Techniques
- Finger Numbers and Octave Distances

In this section, children will explore the foundational elements of piano playing, including the symbols, hand positions, and notes, setting the stage for successful learning.

## Notes on the Piano — 57

- Reading Piano Key Notes
- Locating Notes on the Keyboard

Kids will learn to connect written music with the piano keyboard, developing a practical understanding of their instrument that will enhance their playing skills.

## Note Values and Rhythm — 73

- Understanding Note Values and Rests
- Fundamentals of Rhythm Counting

This section introduces children to the values of notes and rests, and teaches them how different note values work together to create rhythm, a key aspect of piano playing.

# Introduction

***Welcome to a World of Music and Fun!***

Music is more than just a skill; it's a journey of creativity, expression, and joy. Whether you're a parent, a teacher, or a young learner, "Easy Piano Learning for Kids: Master Notes, Keys, and Rhythms with Fun and Simple Exercises" is your perfect companion on this exciting adventure. This book is designed to make learning the piano not only easy but also incredibly fun, ensuring that every child discovers the magic of music while developing essential skills that will last a lifetime.

In this book, you will embark on a musical adventure that seamlessly blends foundational music notation with engaging, hands-on activities. The lessons are carefully structured to build a strong understanding of piano fundamentals, from the basics of piano symbols to the intricacies of rhythm and note values. But more than that, this book is about making learning enjoyable. We believe that when learning is fun, it becomes a natural part of a child's world, fostering a lifelong love for music.

The journey begins with **Learning Notes**, where children will explore the foundational elements of piano playing. They'll learn about the various piano symbols that are the building blocks of music, as well as the correct hand positions for both the left and right hands. Understanding the layout of line and space notes, the roles of the bass and treble clefs, and memorization techniques for note names will empower young pianists to read music with confidence. Additionally, they'll be introduced to finger numbers and octave distances, essential concepts that help in navigating the piano keyboard with ease.

Once the foundation is set, we move on to **Notes on the Piano**. In this section, children will make the crucial connection between written music and the physical keyboard. They'll learn to read piano key notes and locate them on the keyboard, bridging the gap between theory and practice. This hands-on approach ensures that children not only understand the notes but also feel comfortable playing them, turning sheet music into beautiful melodies.

Understanding rhythm is a vital part of playing any musical instrument, and the section on **Note Values and Rhythm** is dedicated to this important aspect. Here, children will be introduced to the values of notes and rests, learning how different note durations work together to create rhythm. Through fun and simple exercises, they will grasp the fundamentals of rhythm counting, an essential skill that will help them play music with the right timing and flow.

Throughout the book, each chapter is designed to be both educational and enjoyable, with a mix of written explanations and practical exercises. We understand that children learn best when they are engaged, so we have included a variety of activities that cater to different learning styles. Whether it's through games, drawing, or playing, every lesson is an opportunity for creativity and discovery.

As you guide your child or student through this book, you'll find that "Easy Piano Learning for Kids" is more than just a piano method; it's an invitation to explore the world of music in a way that is accessible, fun, and rewarding. By the end of this journey, young pianists will have mastered the basics of piano playing and gained a deep appreciation for music that will inspire them for years to come.

So, open this book, turn to the first page, and let the musical adventure begin. The joy of learning the piano is just a few notes away!

Happy Playing!
Clara Forte

# LEARNING NOTES

# LESSON: Meaning of Basic Music Symbols

**STAFF LINES**

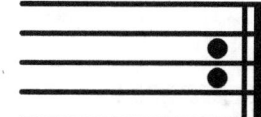

Note on line

Note in Space

5 lines
4 spaces

**REPEAT**

**BAR LINE**

Divides staff
into measures

**BASS CLEF**

Left Hand

**TREBLE CLEF**

Right Hand

**SHARP**

Raise half step

**FLAT**

Lower half step

Easy Piano Learning for Kids | 7

 **Color the hand that should play the note**

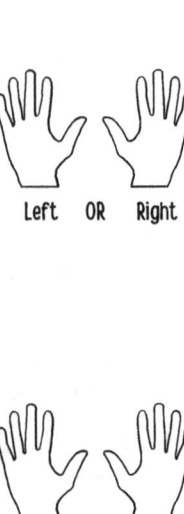
Left   OR   Right

Left   OR   Right

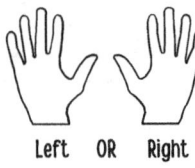
Left   OR   Right

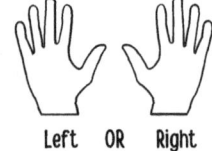
Left   OR   Right

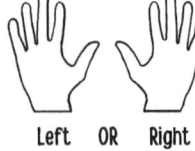
Left   OR   Right

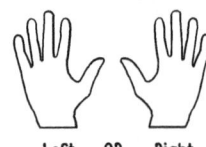
Left   OR   Right

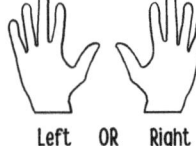
Left   OR   Right

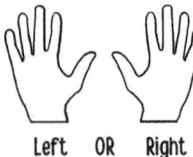
Left   OR   Right

8 | Easy Piano LEARNING for Kids

 Color the balloon RED if the note is on a line and BLUE if the note is on a space

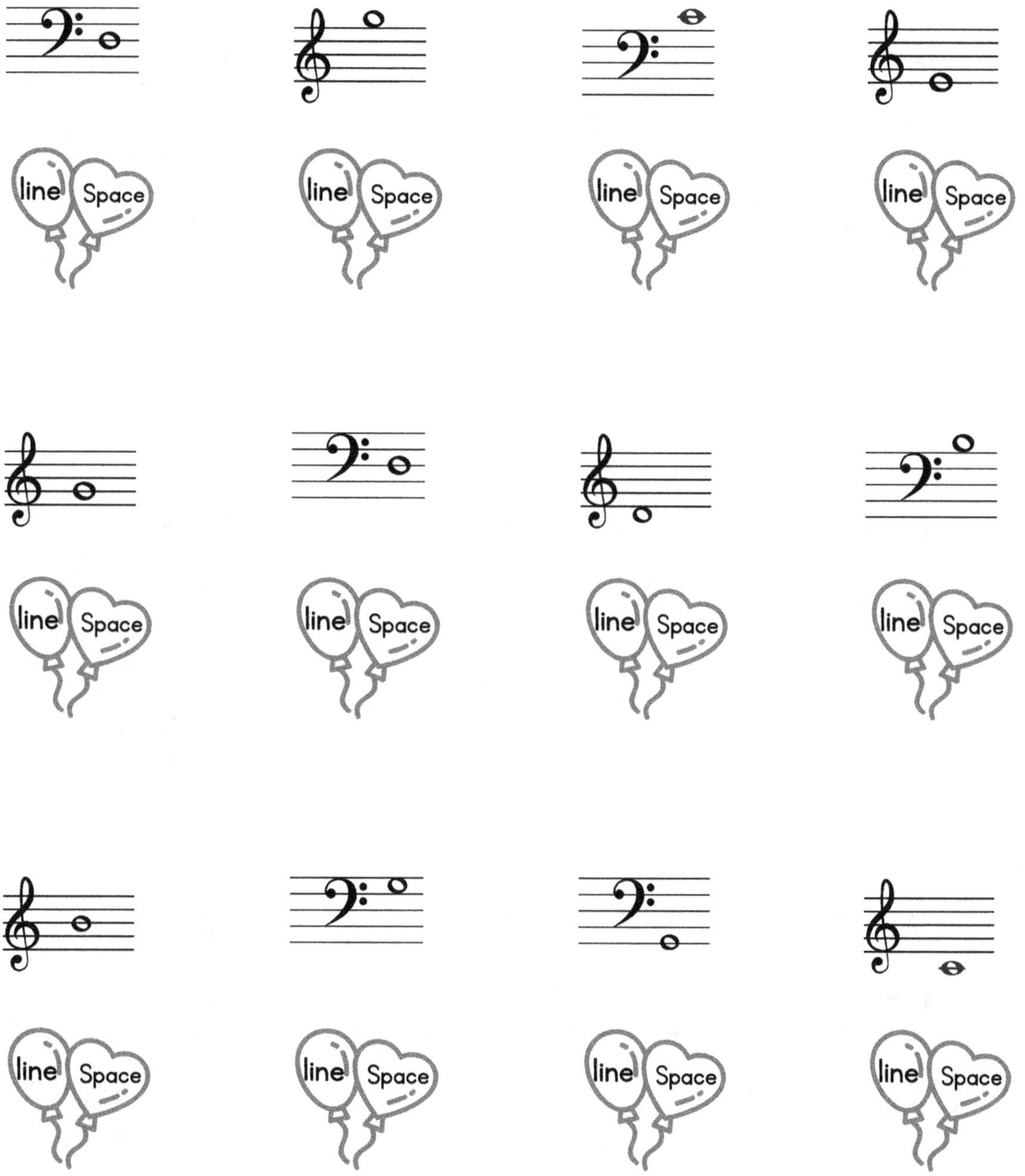

Circle the hand that should play the note

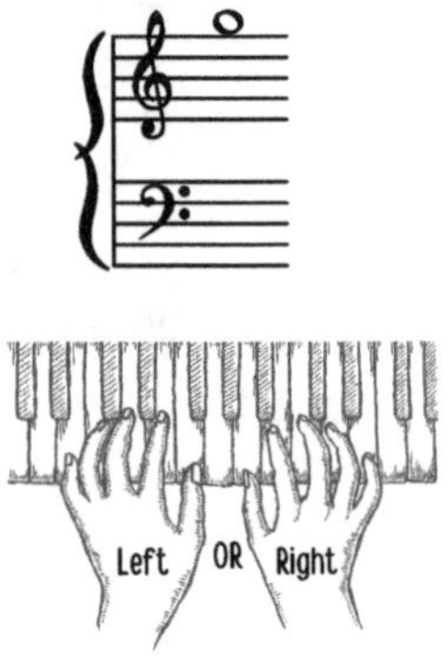

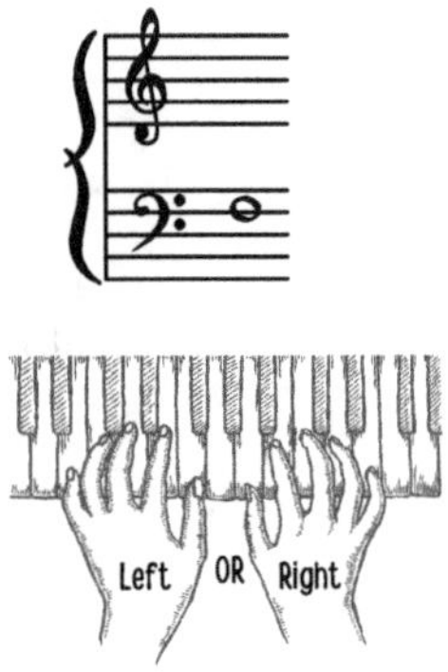

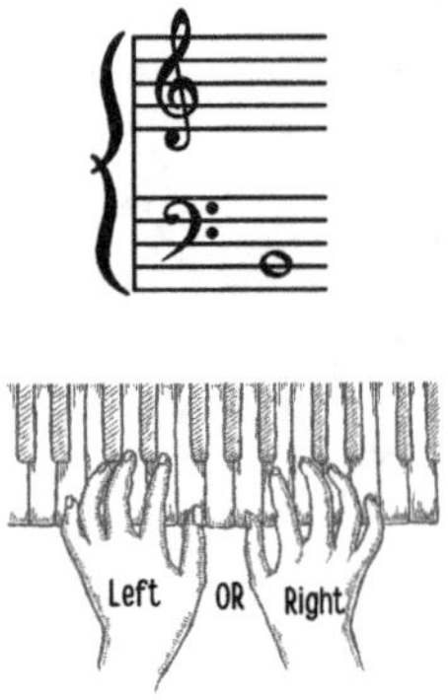

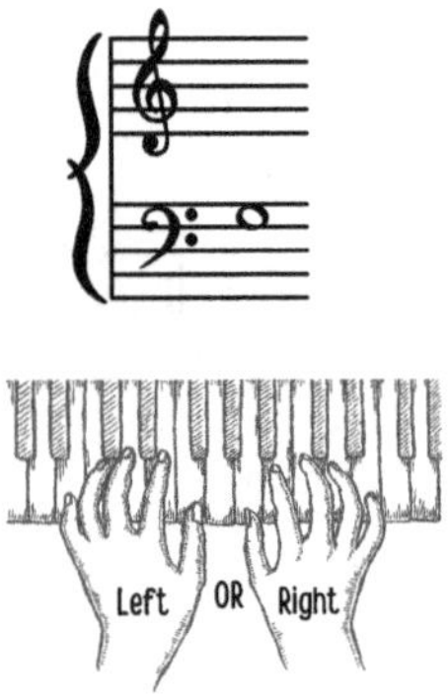

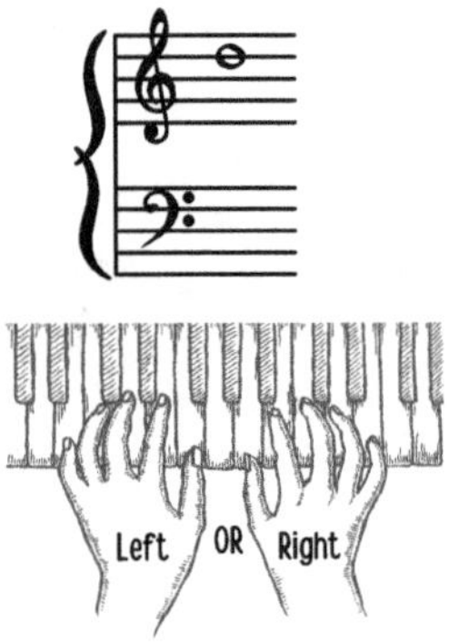

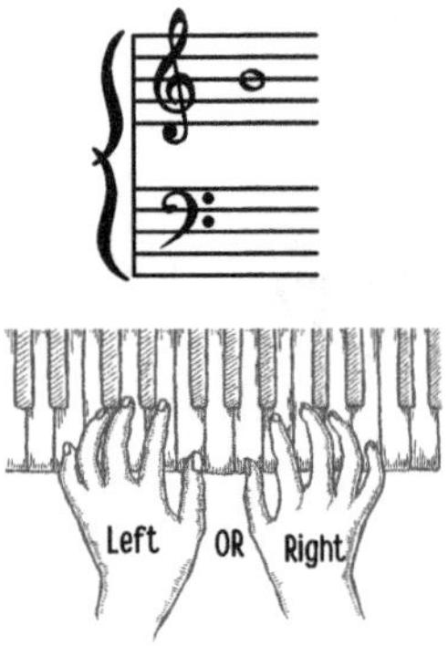

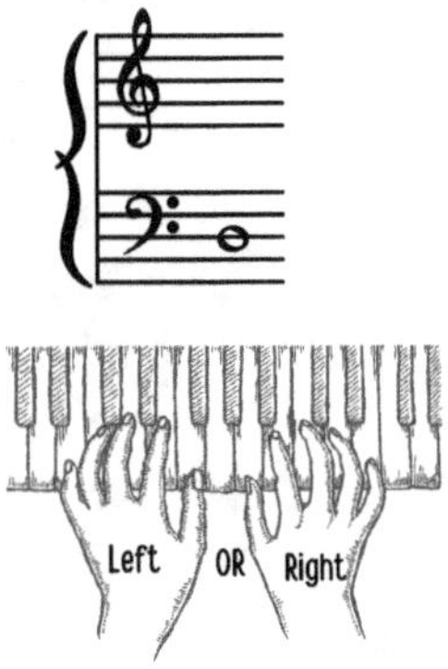

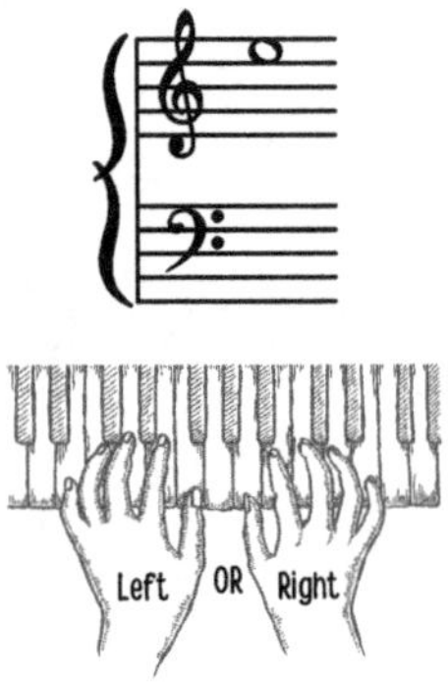

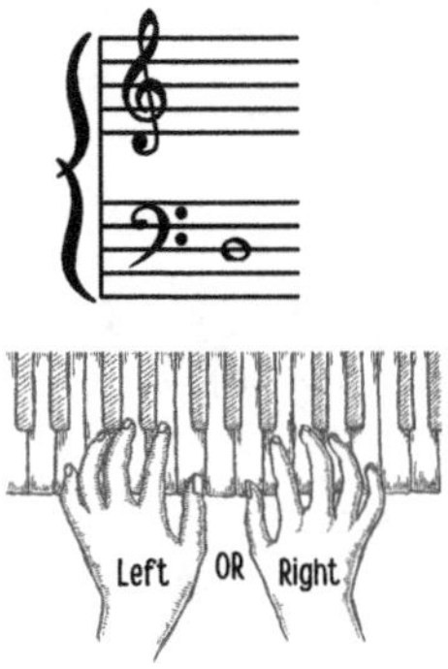

 **Color the balloon in RED if you find a Treble Clef or in YELLOW if you find a Bass Clef**

 Color the balloon in GREEN if you find a note on a line and in RED if you find a note on a space

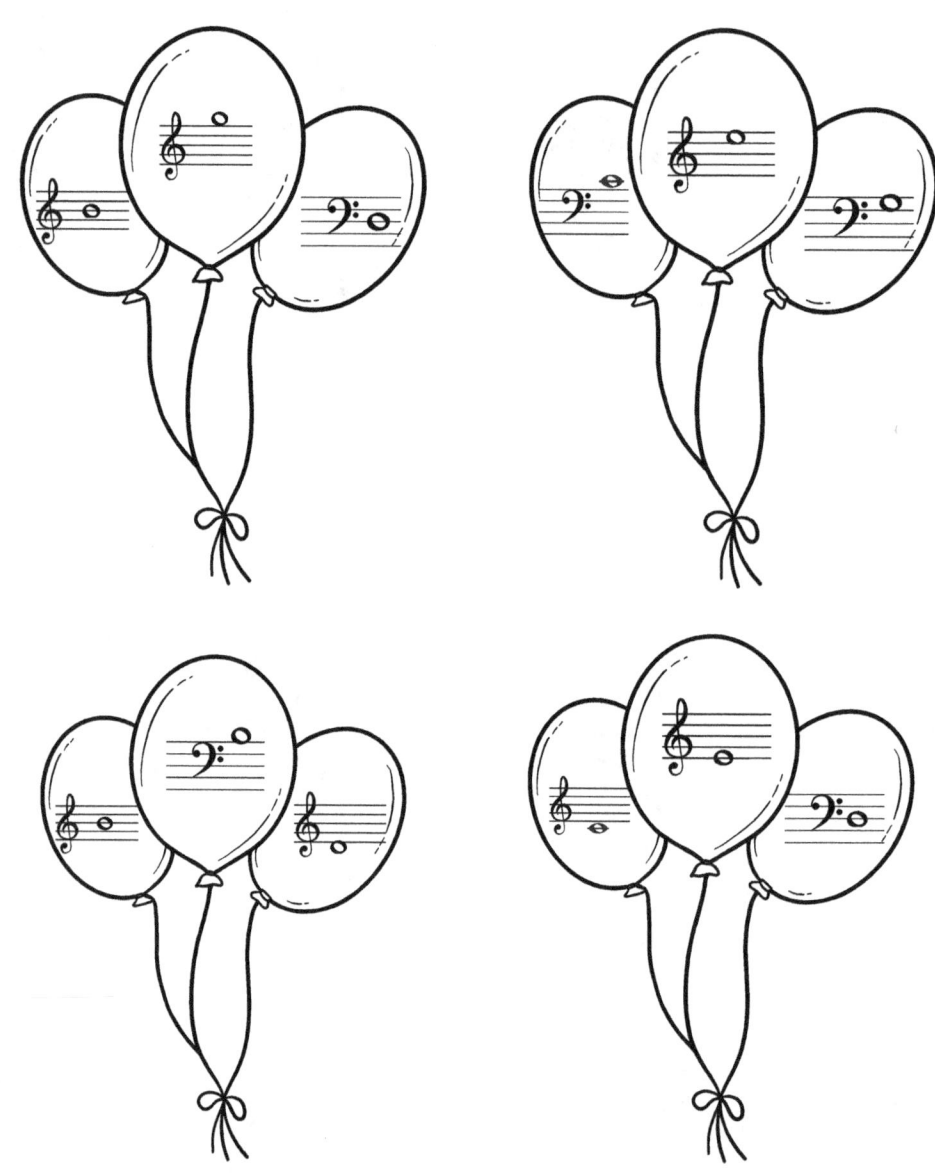

# LESSON: Musical Hands Configuration

In music, finger numbers are essential for indicating which finger should play a particular note on an instrument, such as the piano or guitar or violin.

For piano, the numbering system typically assigns the thumb as finger 1, the index finger as 2, the middle finger as 3, the ring finger as 4, and the little finger as 5 for both hands as shown below:

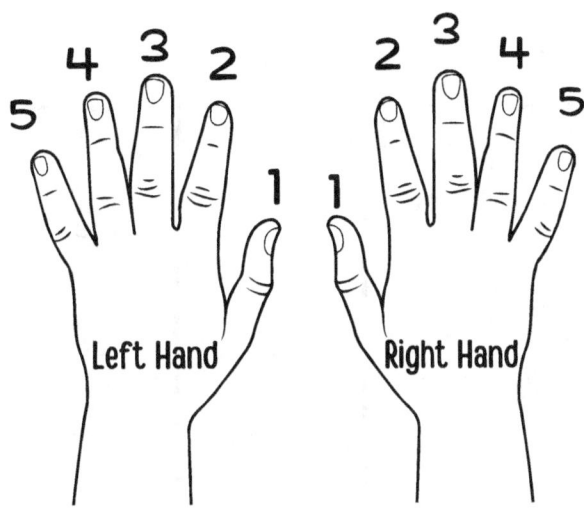

 **Draw a line to match each finger to the right number**

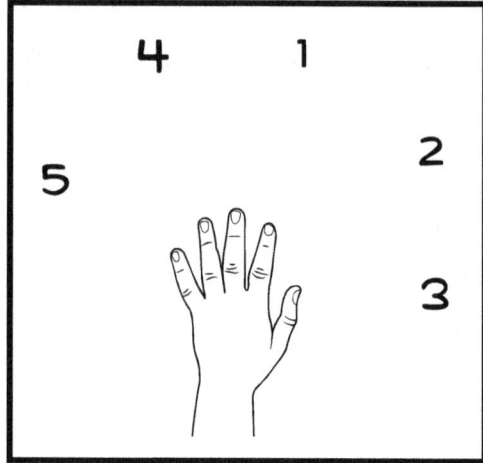

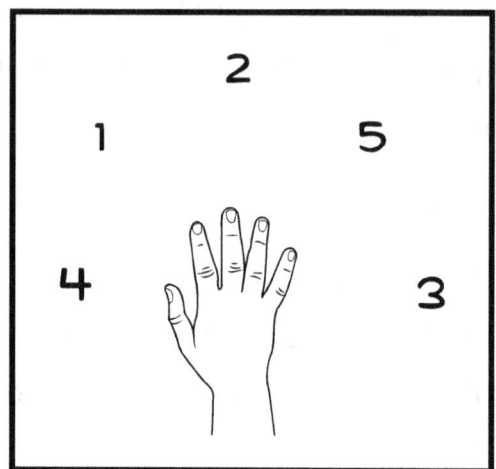

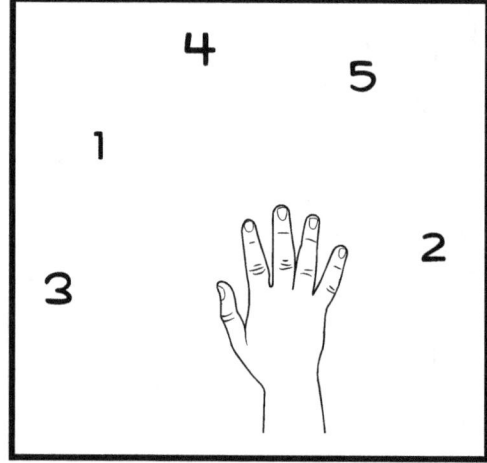

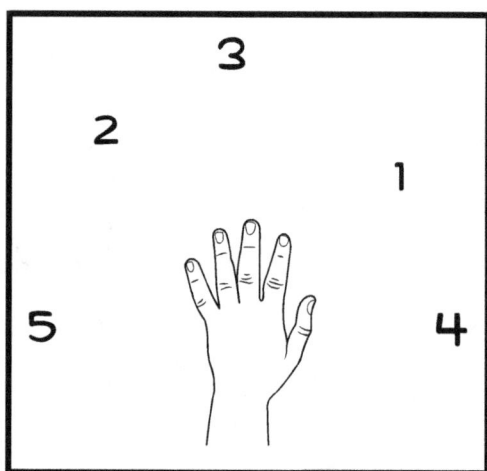

 **Write the correct finger number where the star is located**

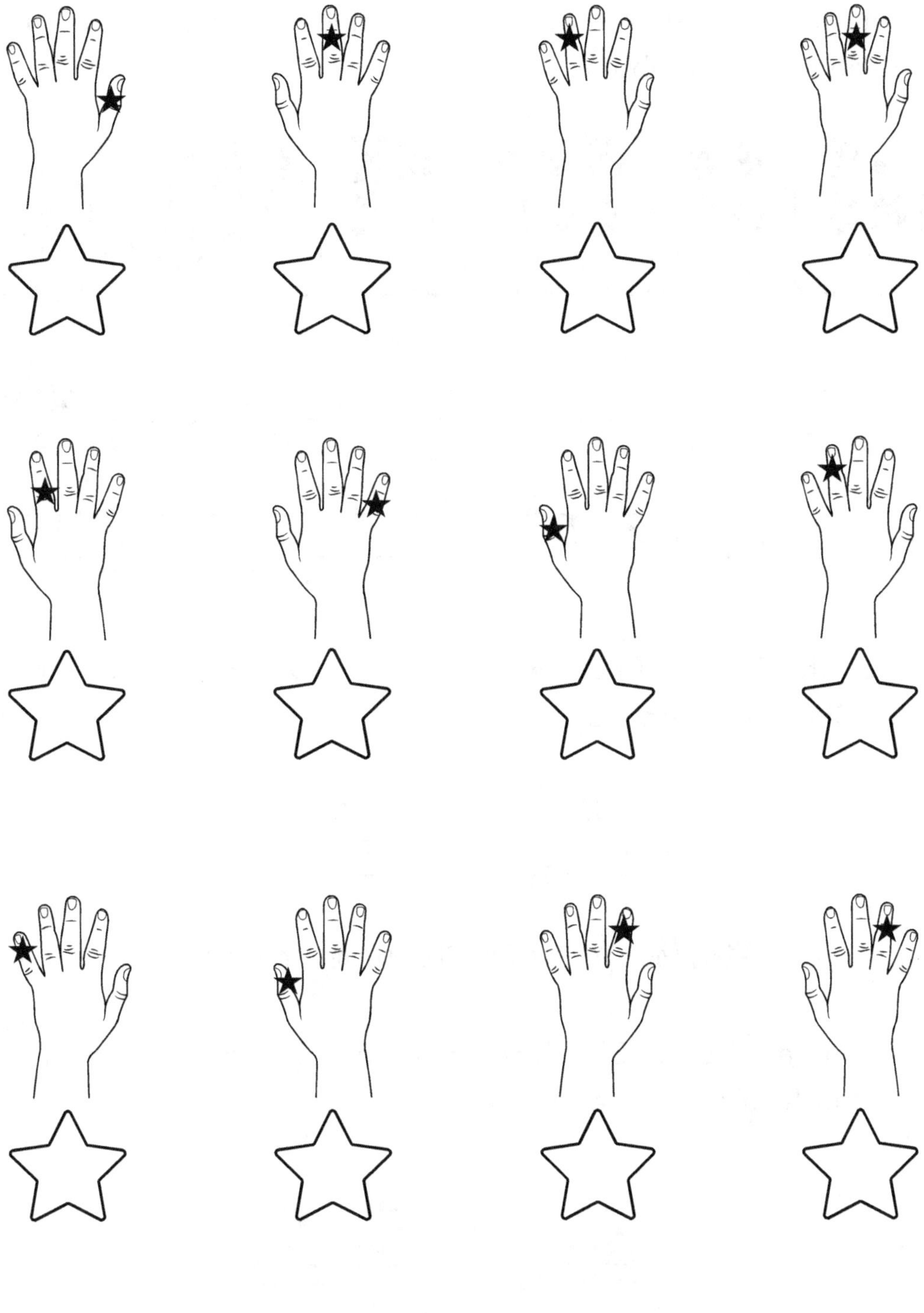

# LESSON

Piano keys are labeled with letters A,B,C,D,E,F,G repeated in a pattern across the keyboard. Each octave on the piano consists of these seven letters, and the sequence starts again with A after G, creating multiple sets of these notes across the entire piano keyboard.

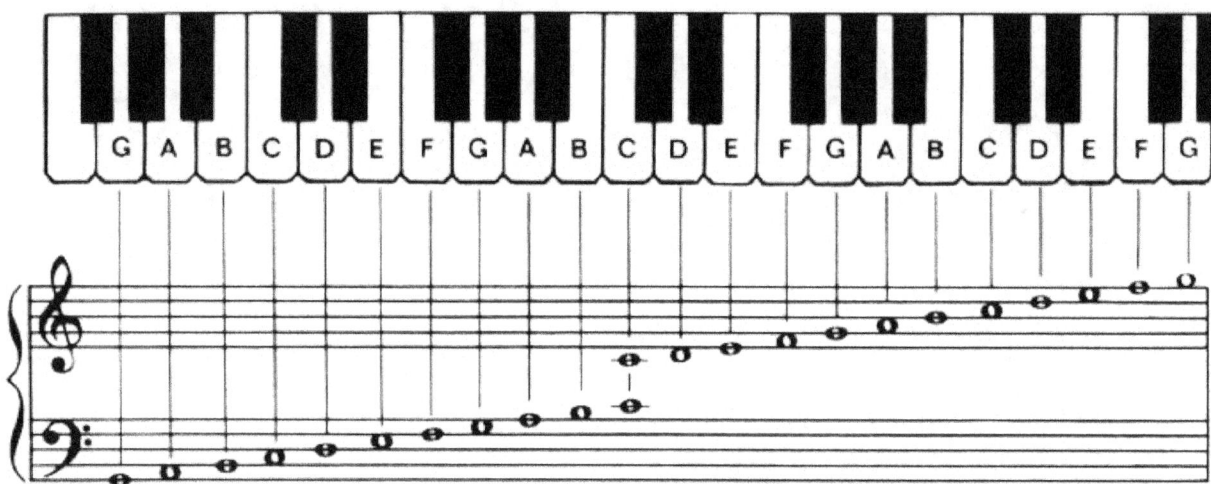

Each note on the Bass Clef has its matching octave note in a different location on the Bass Clef. See example:

**These two notes are G on Bass Clef with one octave distance**

Each note on the Treble Clef has its matching octave note in a different location on the Treble Clef. See example:

**These two notes are E on Treble Clef with one octave distance**

LESSON: Memorizing Notes

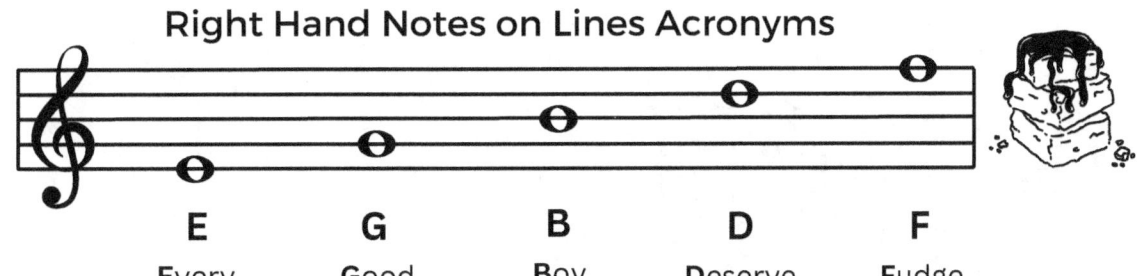

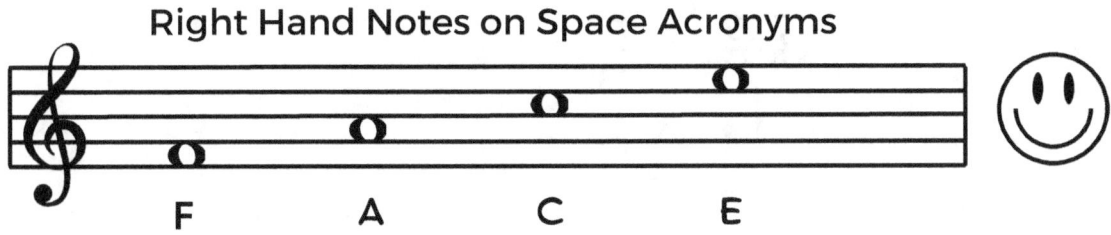

REMEMBER! → For naming the notes on Bass Clef you should:
1- Name it on Treble Clef and then 2- Go two letters up

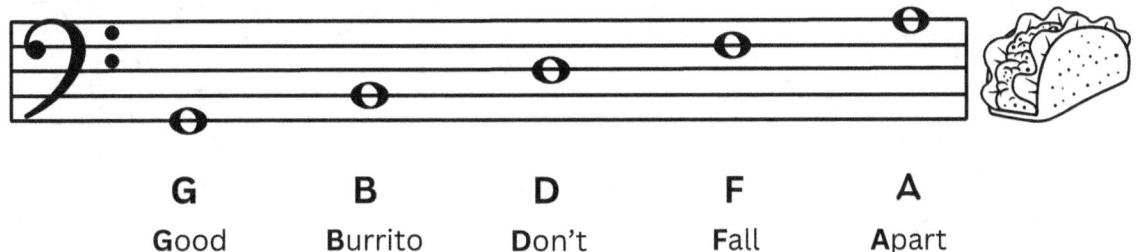

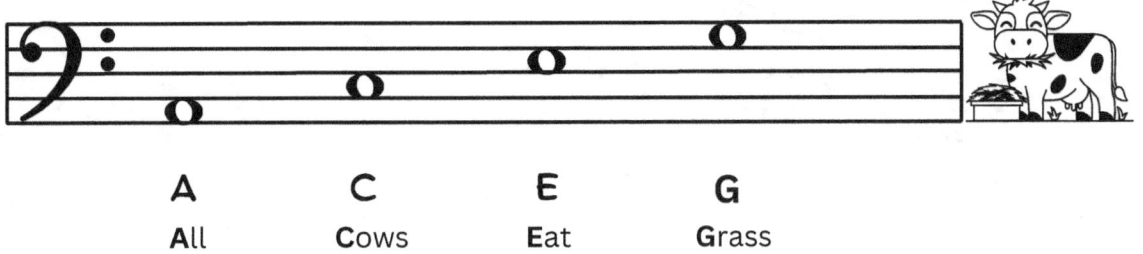

Easy Piano Learning for Kids | 17

**Find each note key on Bass Clef to it's match note**

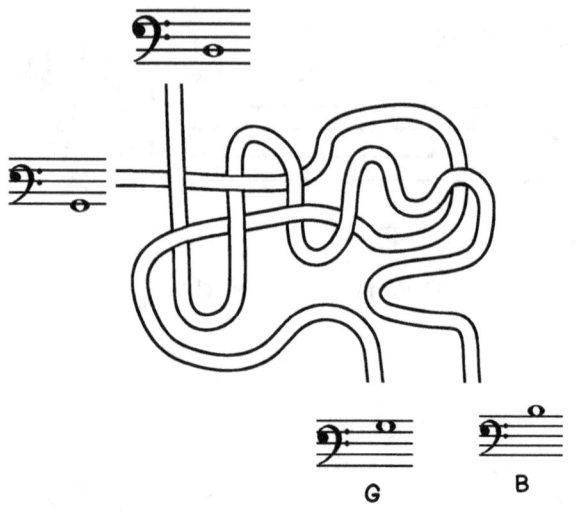

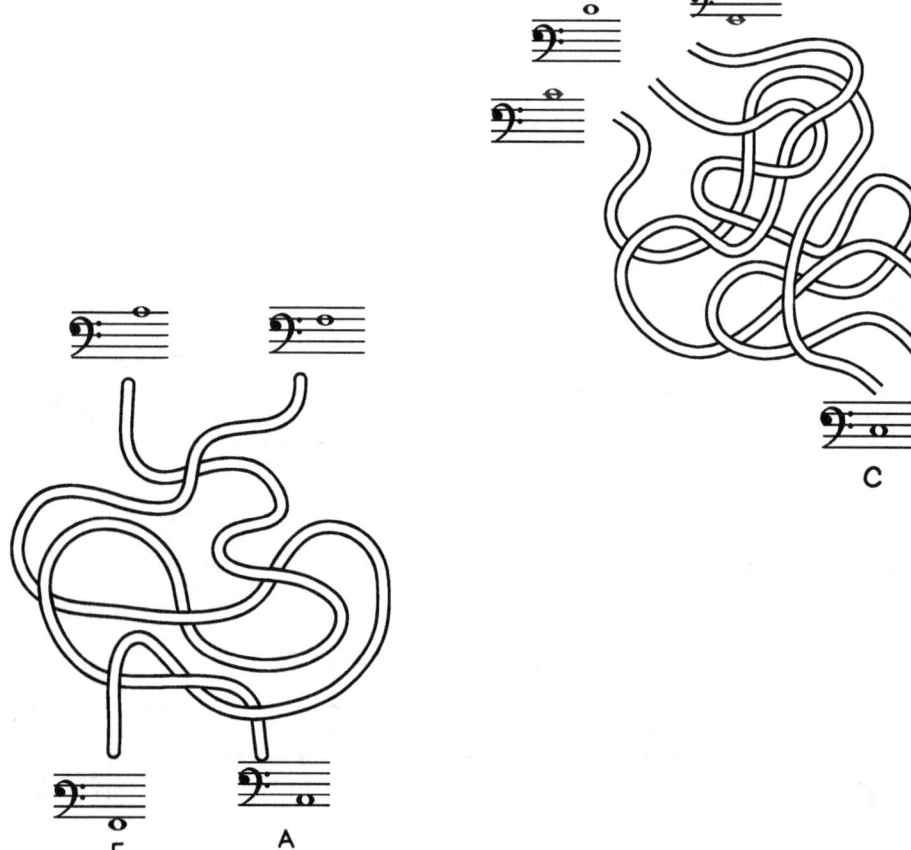

**Find each note key on Treble Clef to it's match note**

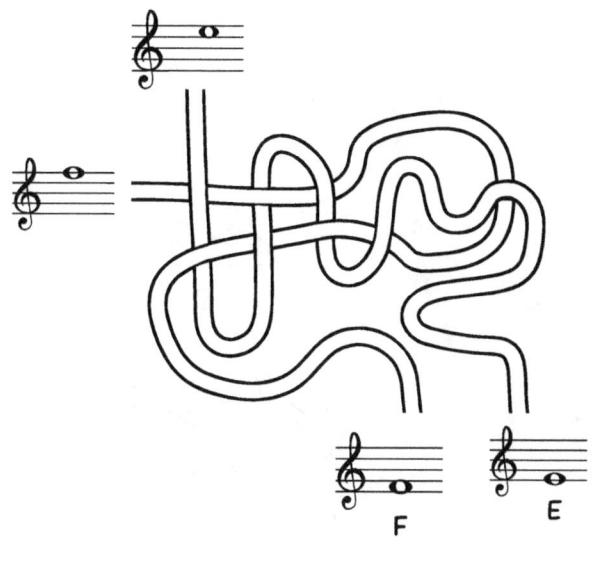

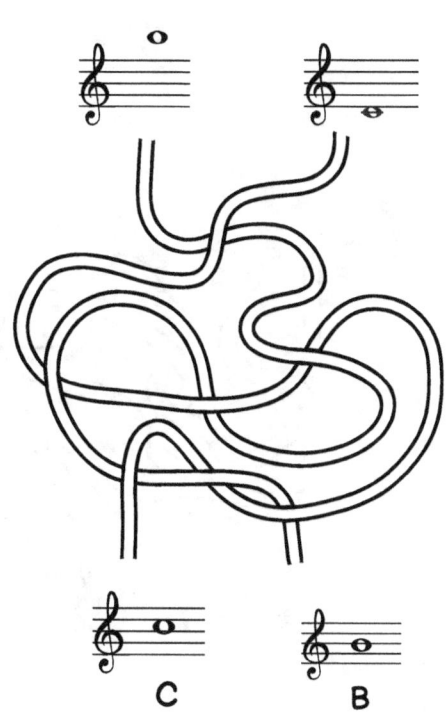

**Find each note key on Bass Clef to it's match note**

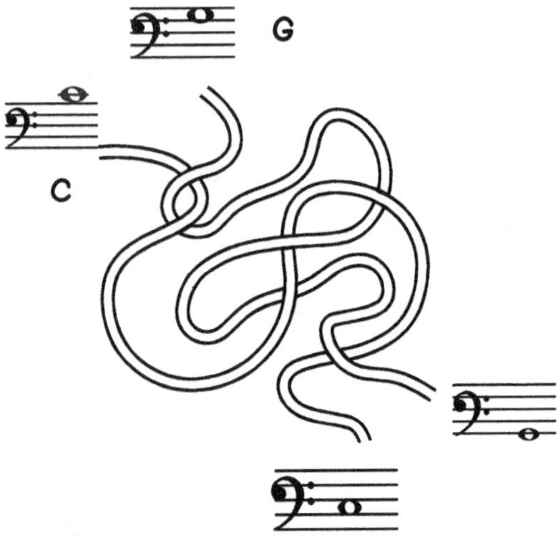

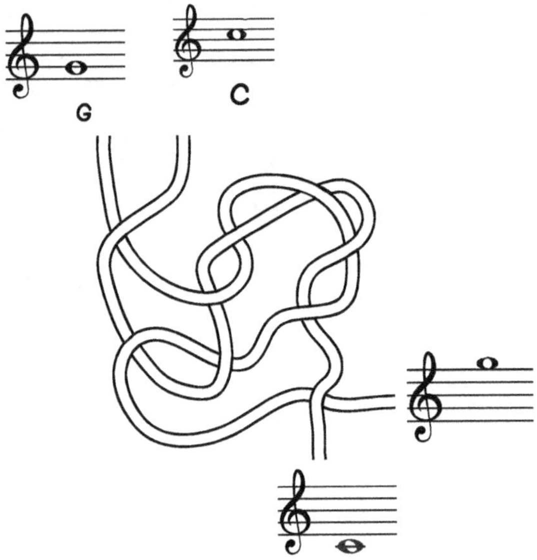

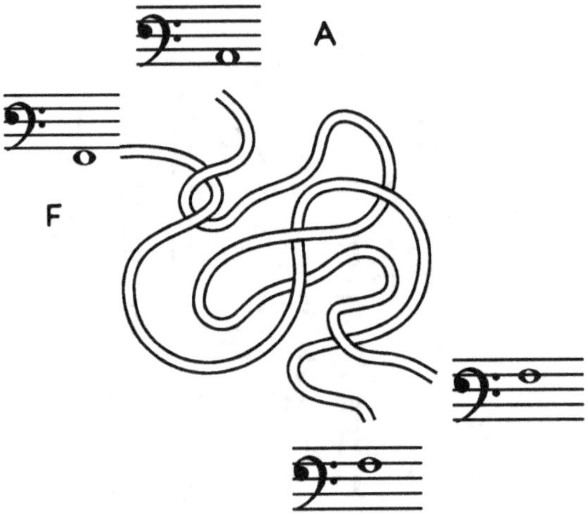

**Write the letter note before and after the note the little bee is carrying**

1-  ____  🐝C  ____  ____  ____  G____

2-  ____  ____  ____  🐝C  ____  ____

3-  ____  F____  ____  ____  ____  🐝C

4-  ____  ____  🐝C  ____  ____  ____

5-  ____  ____  ____  ____  🐝C  ____

Easy Piano Learning for Kids | 21

**Circle all of the Right Hand middle C's**

**Right Hand D:**
Draw a line to match the letter D to each Right Hand D

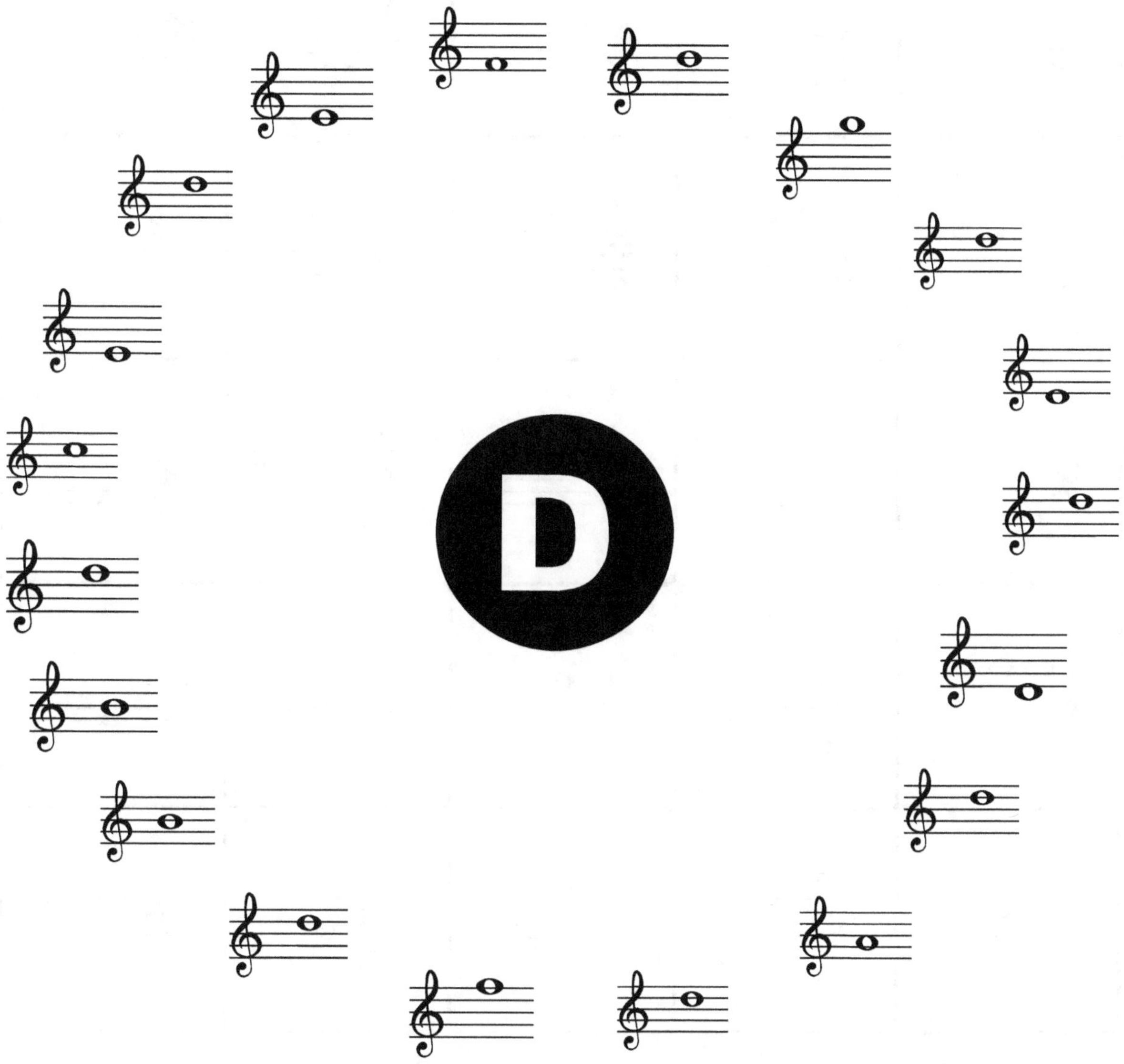

# Right Hand E:
## Color ONLY the squares that contain Right Hand E

**Circle all of the Left Hand middle C's.**

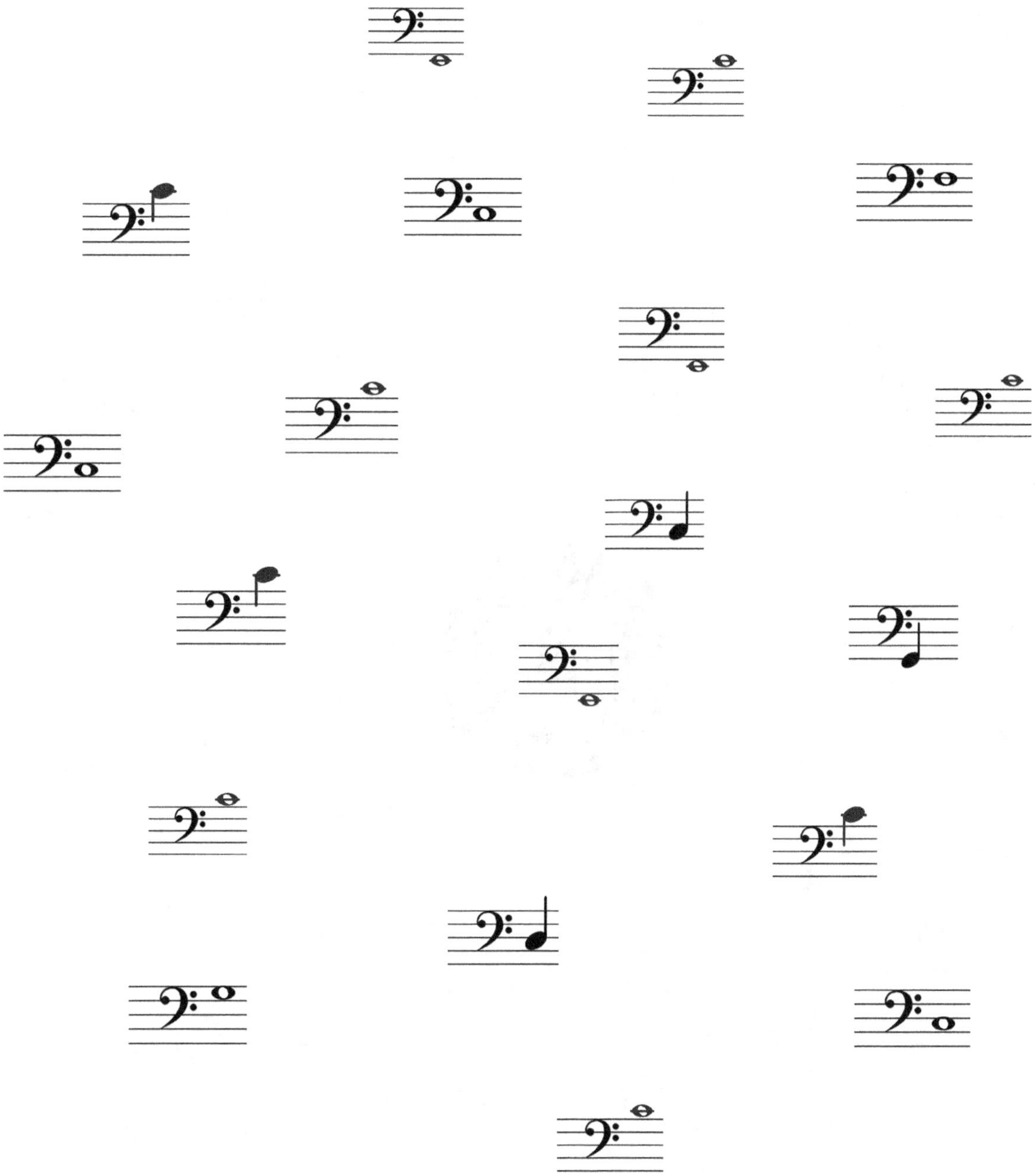

Left Hand D:
Draw a line to match the letter D to each Left Hand D on the staff

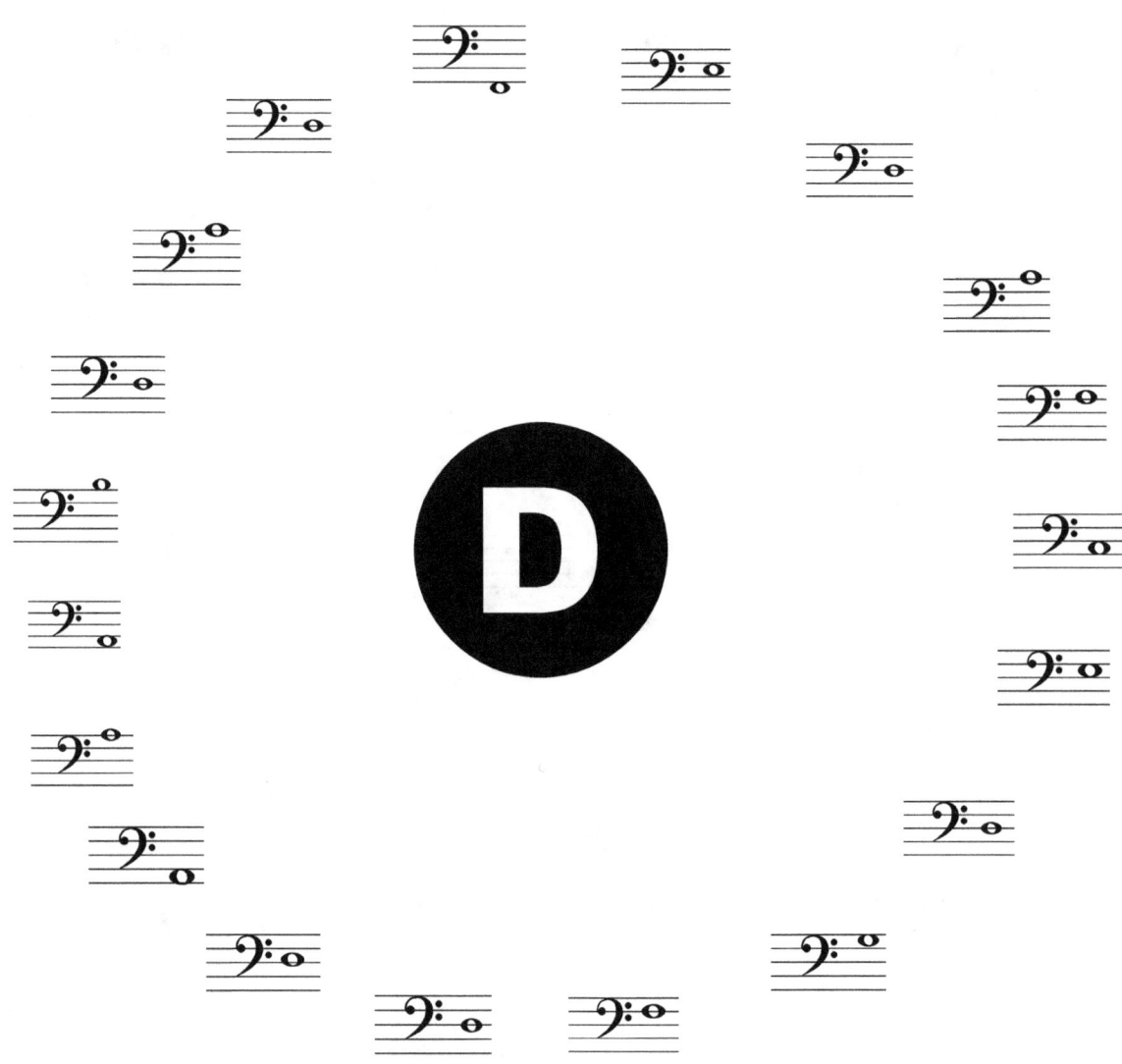

**Left Hand E:**

Color ONLY the squares that contain Left Hand E

 Color the correct note names balloon

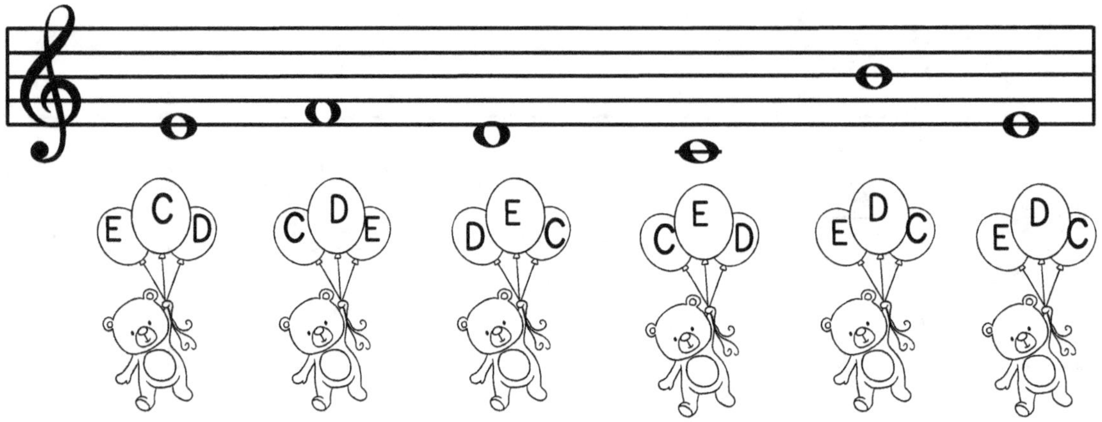

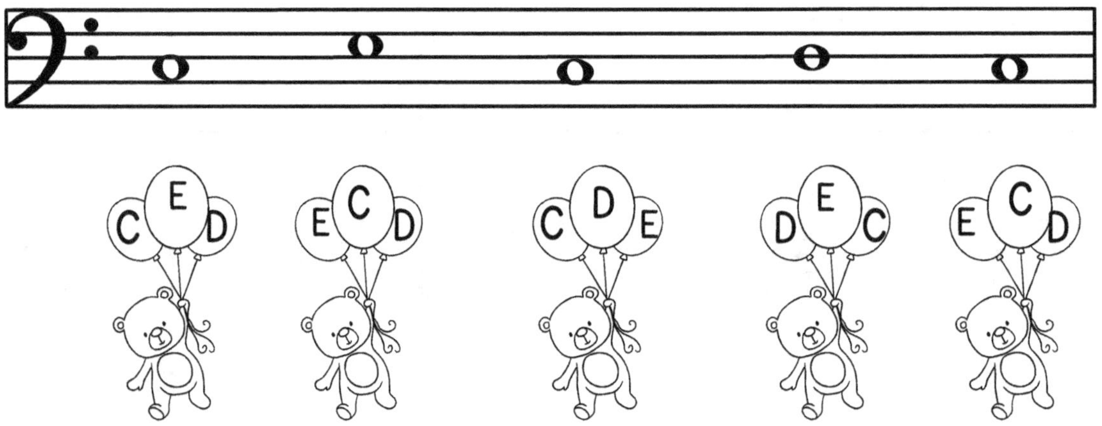

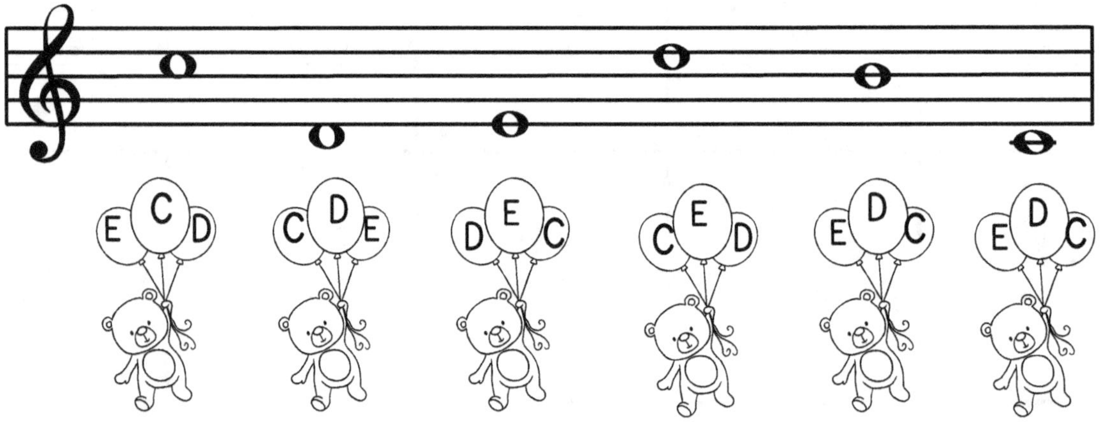

**Write each note of C, D, E name on the shell**

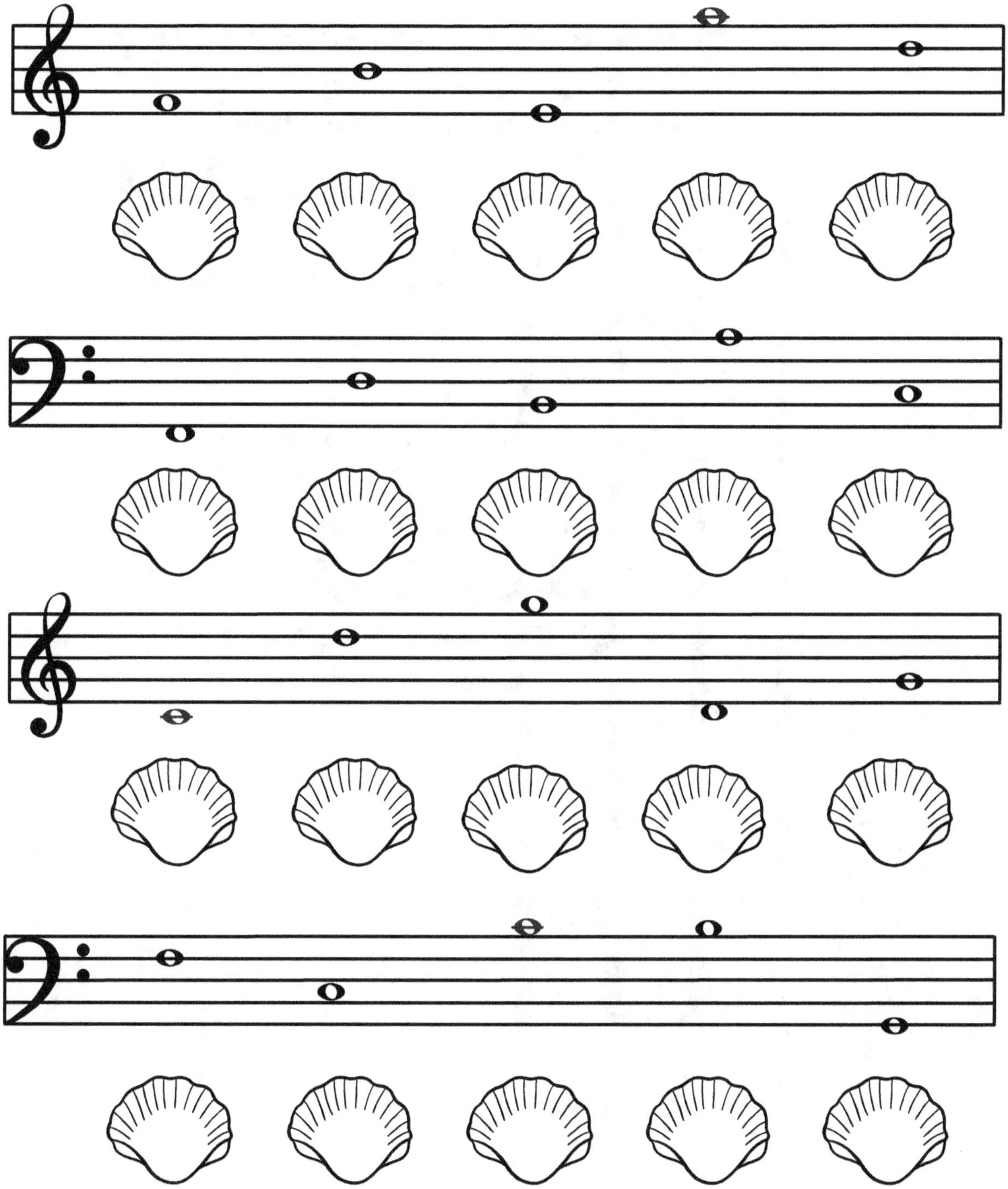

**Follow note F on Treble Clef to help the postman to find the letter F**

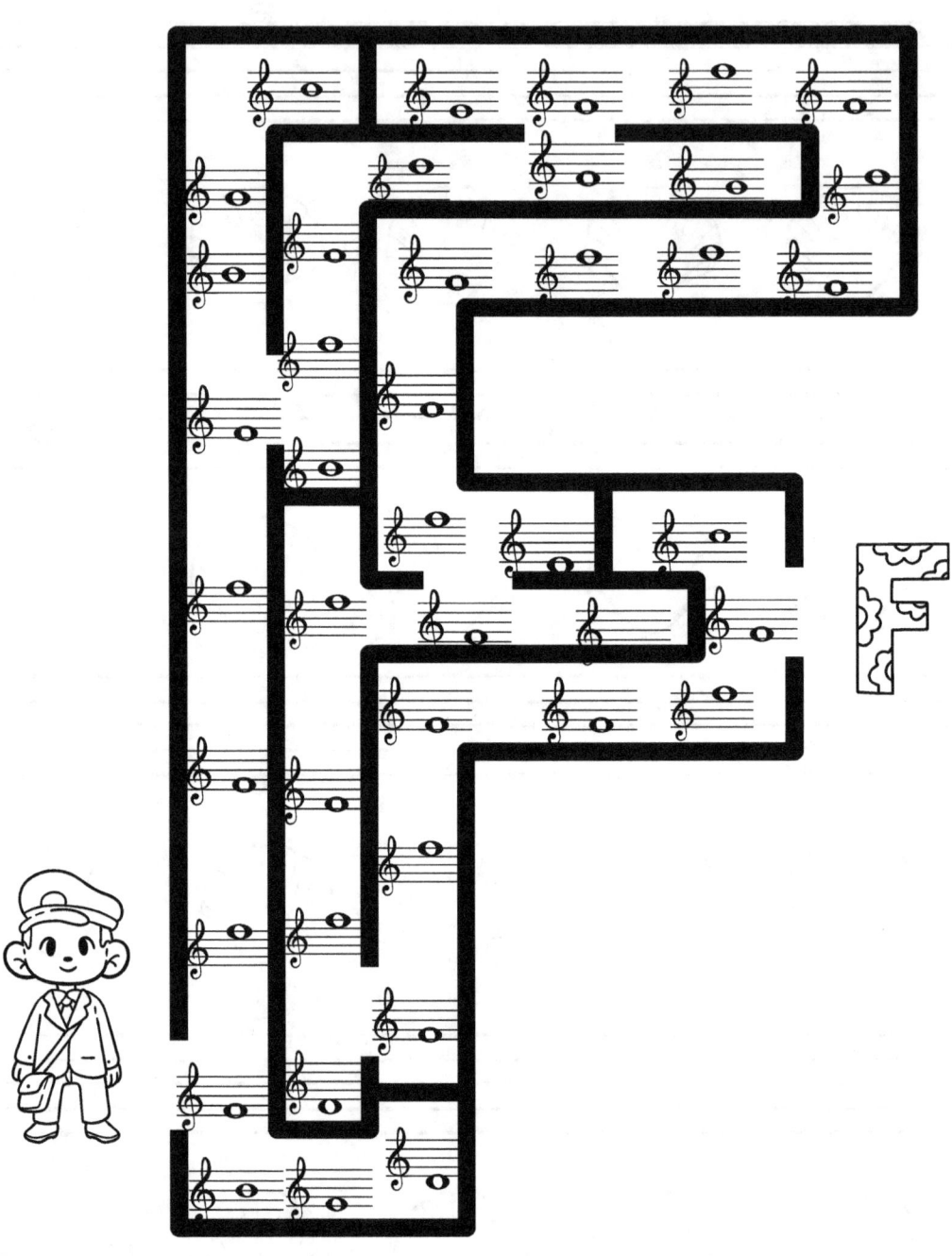

# Circle all of the Right Hand G

**Circle the correct note names**

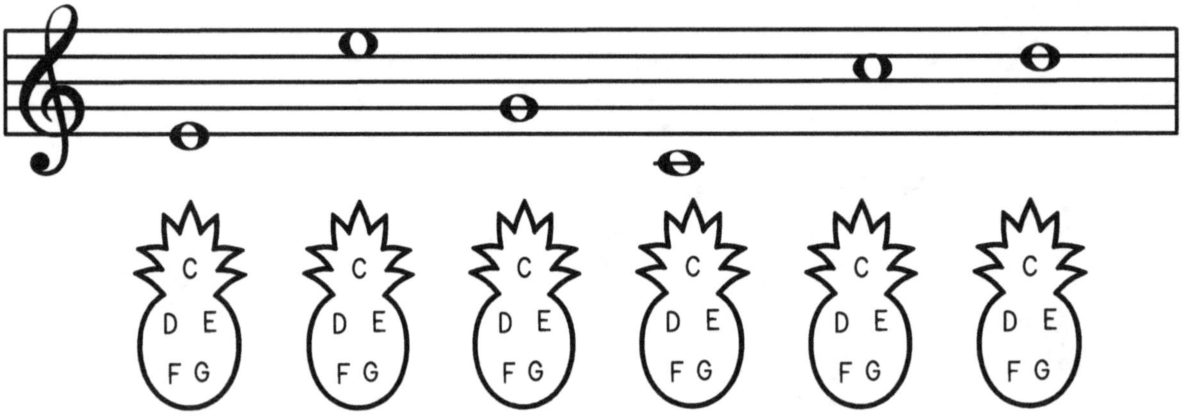

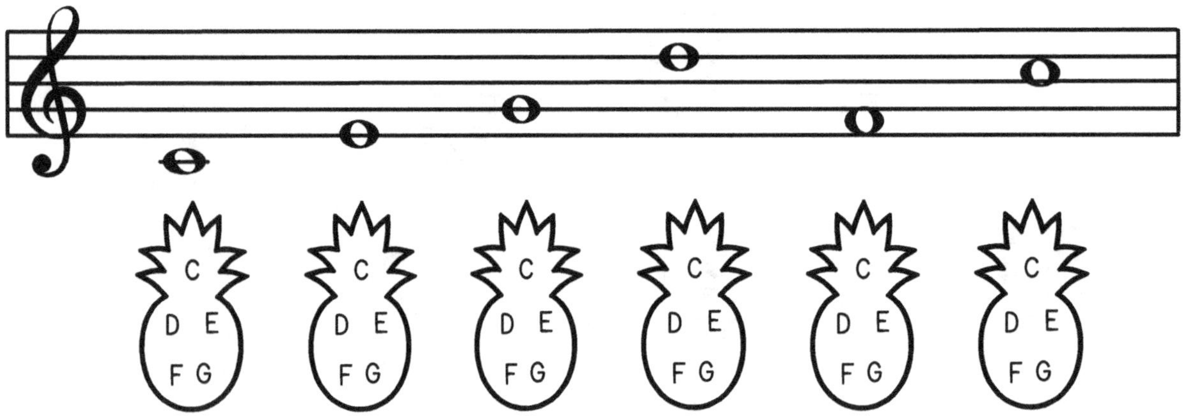

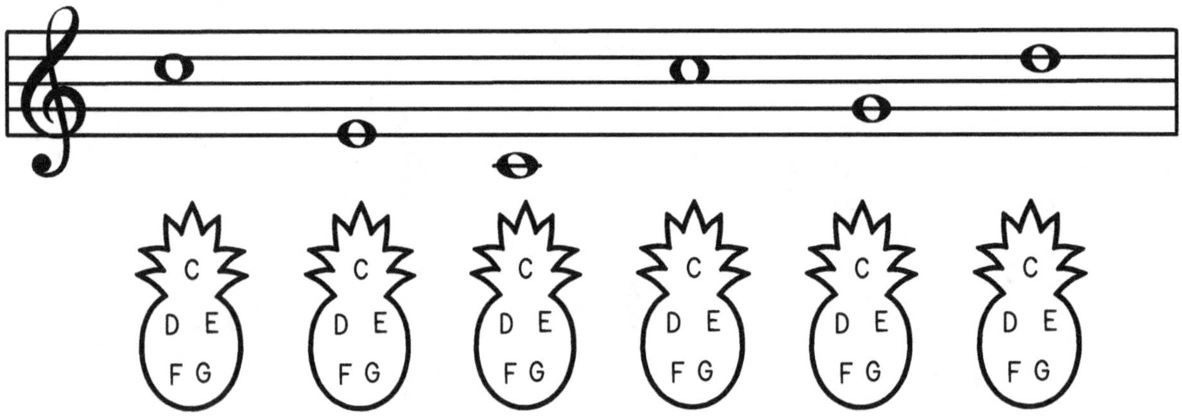

**Follow note G on Bass Clef to help the postman to find the letter G**

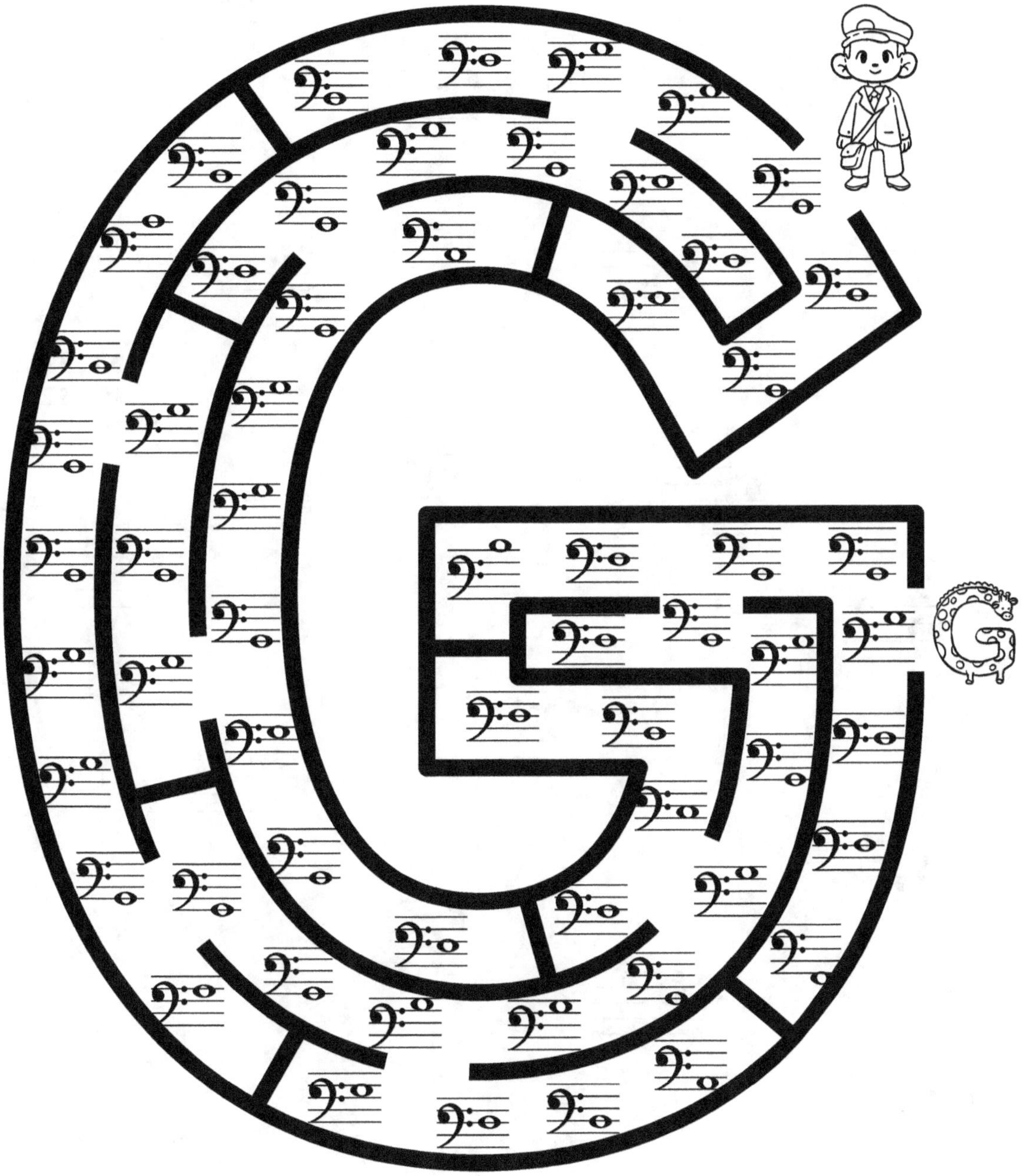

**Left Hand F:**
**Circle all of the Left Hand F's**

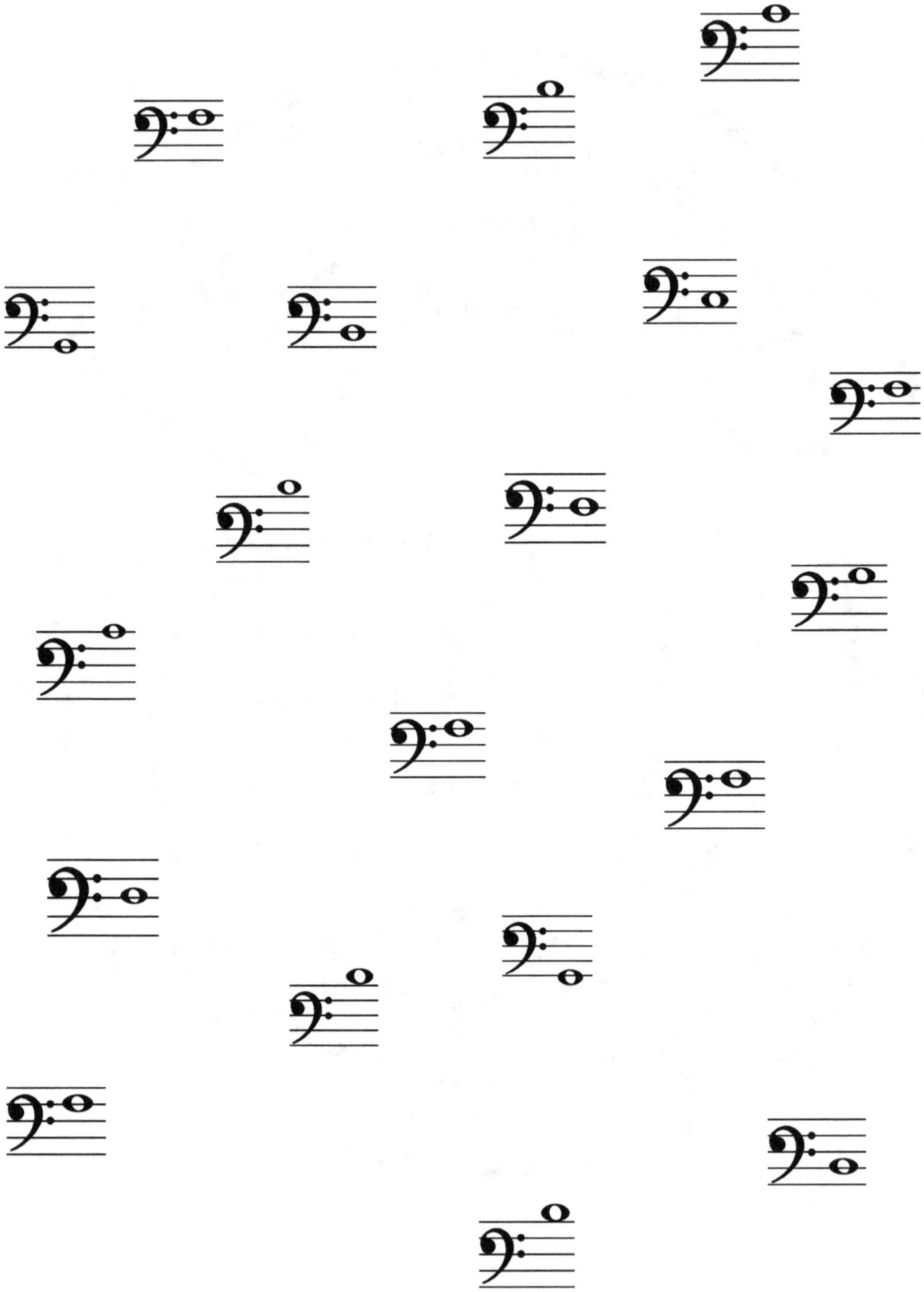

Circle the correct note name

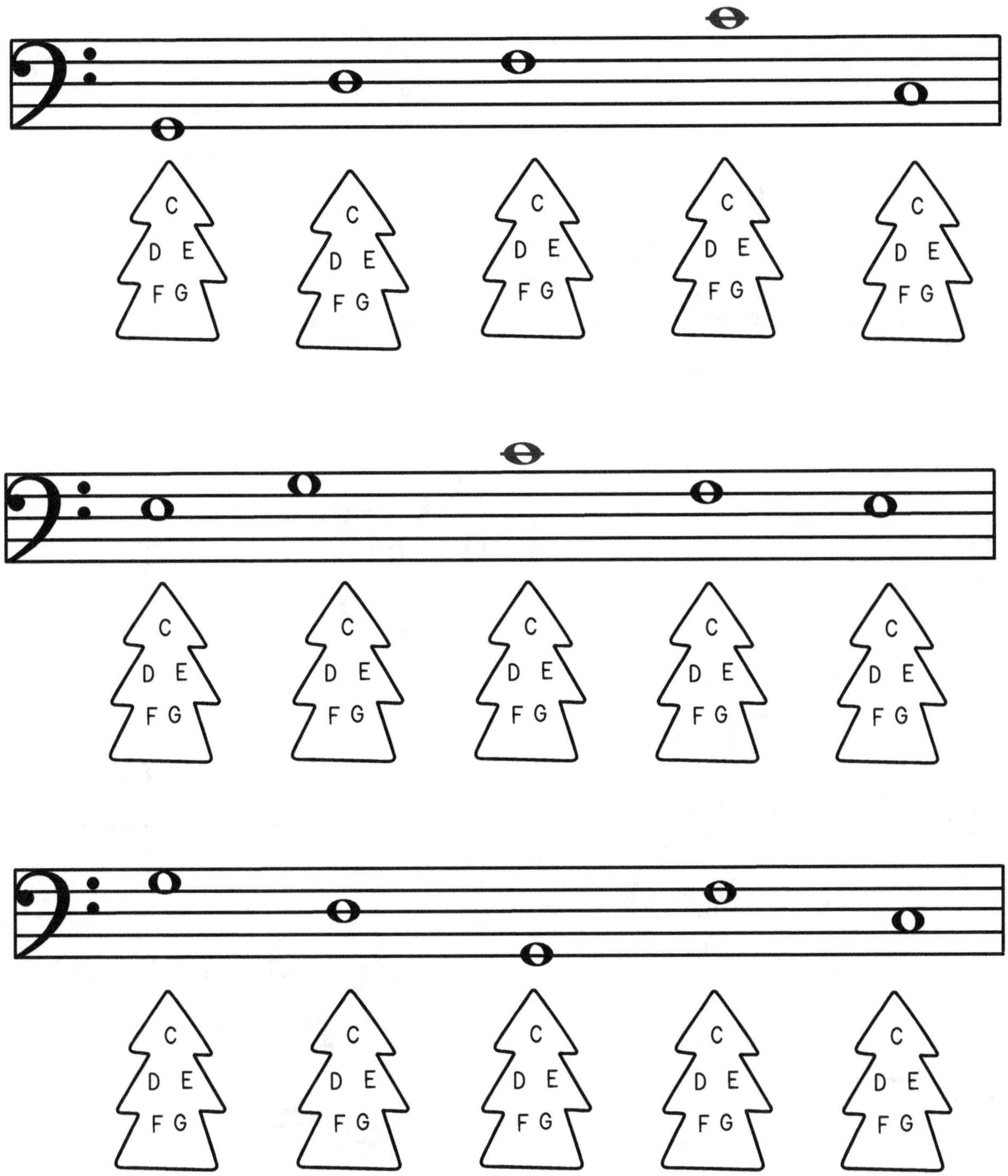

**Write the letter note before and after the note Monkey showing**

1. ---- ---- ---- C ---- ----

2. F ---- ---- G ---- ---- B ----

3. ---- ---- ---- D ---- ---- F

4. ---- C ---- ---- ---- G

5. ---- ---- ---- ---- G ---- A ----

**Left Hand A:**

Color ONLY the squares that contain Left Hand A

Follow note B on Bass Clef to help the postman to find the letter B

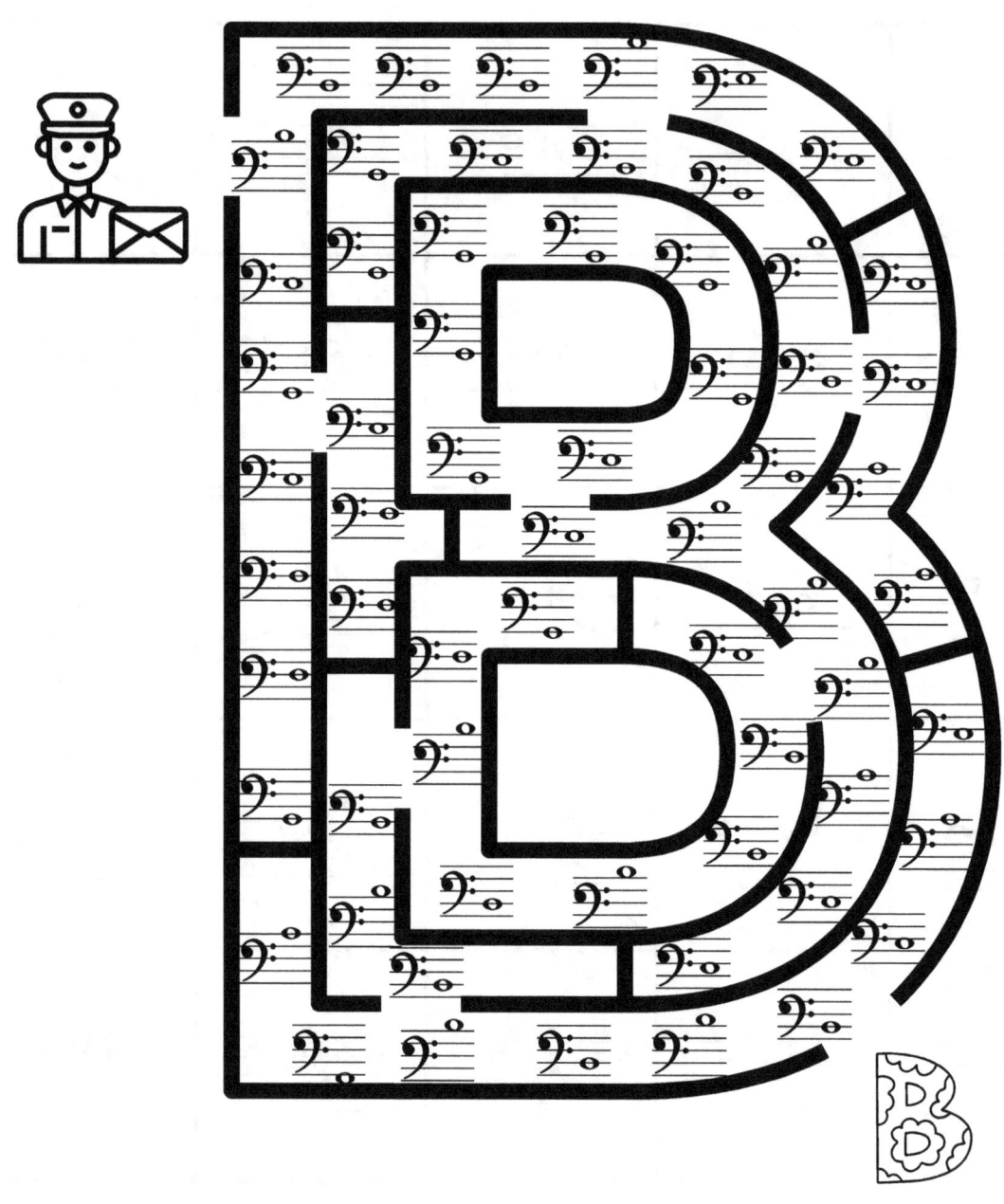

**Right Hand A:**

Draw a line to match the letter A to each Right Hand A.

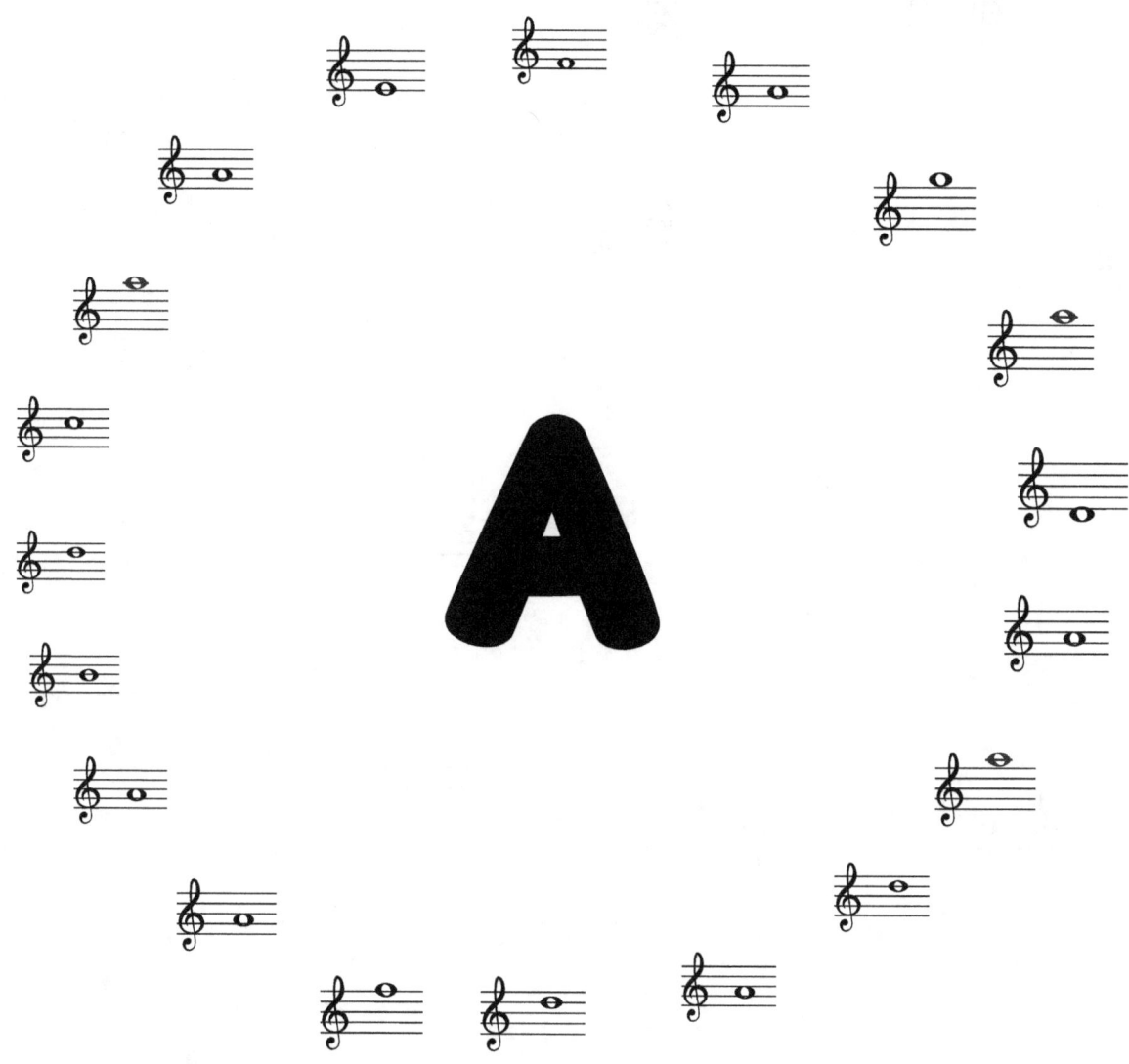

Circle all of the Right Hand B

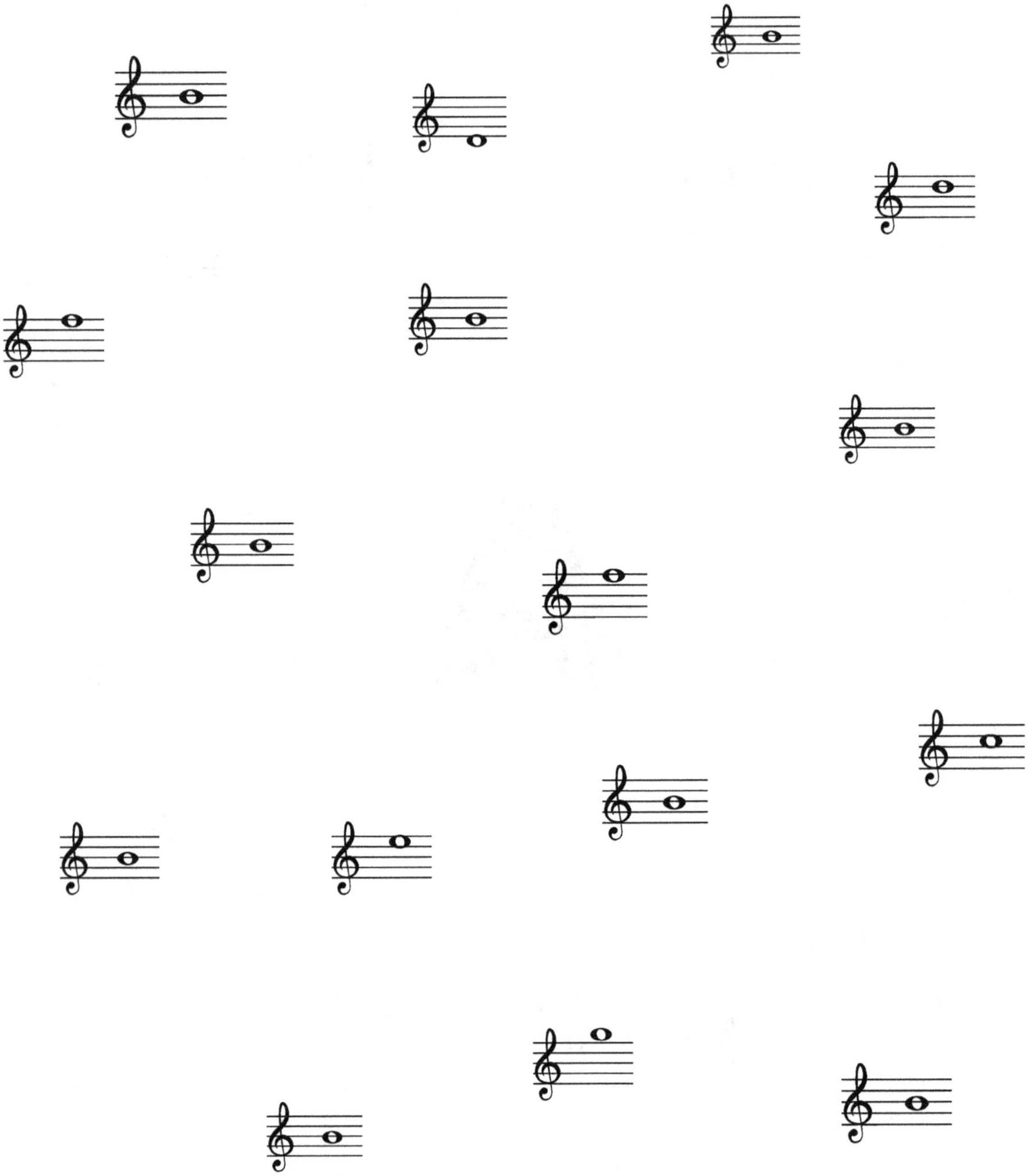

✏️ Write each note name in the sun underneath each note

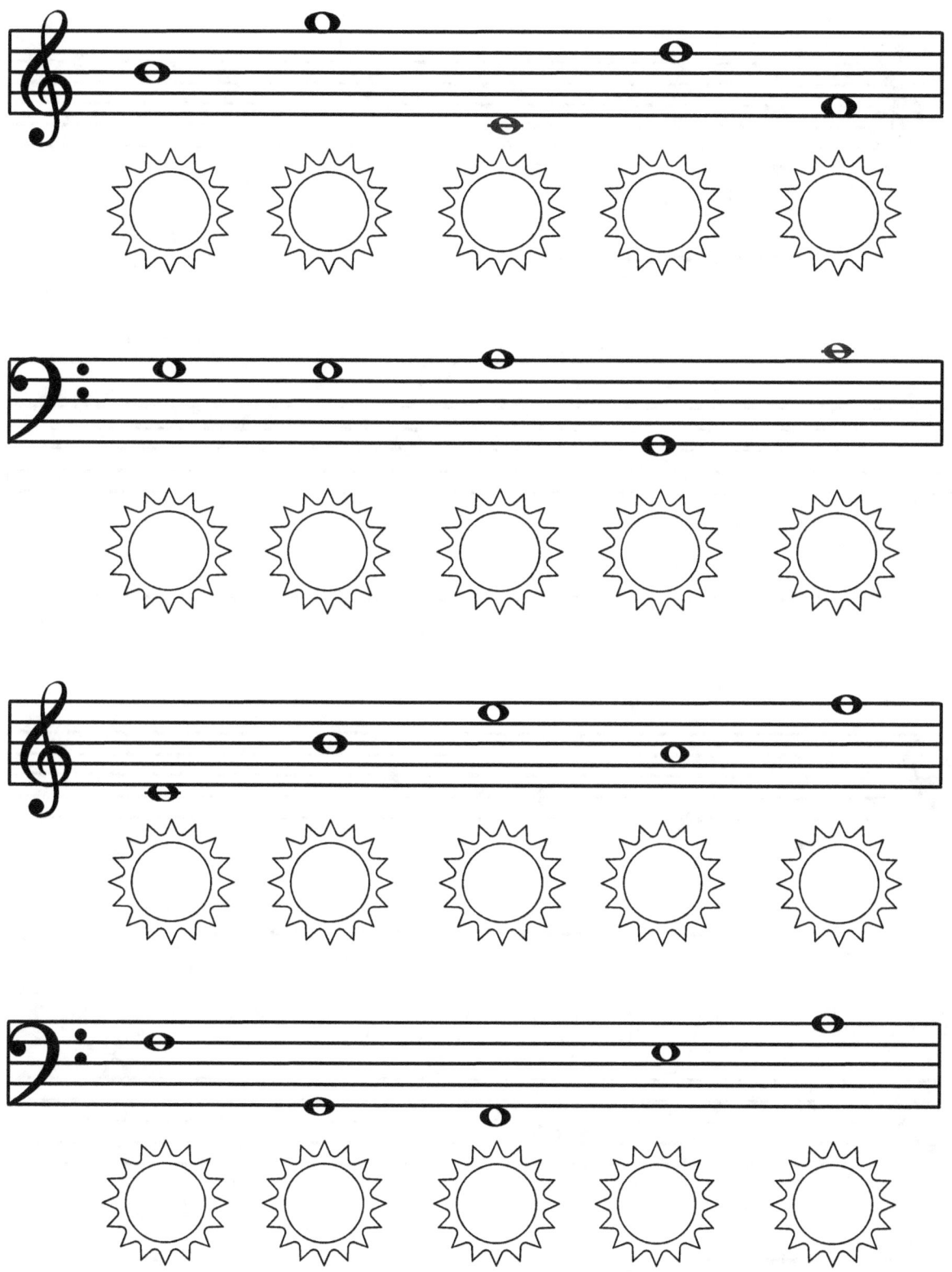

✏️ **Write each note name below it**

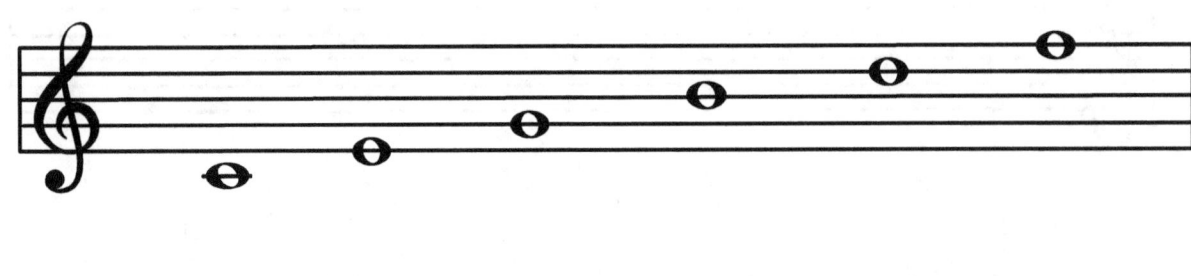

— — — — — — —

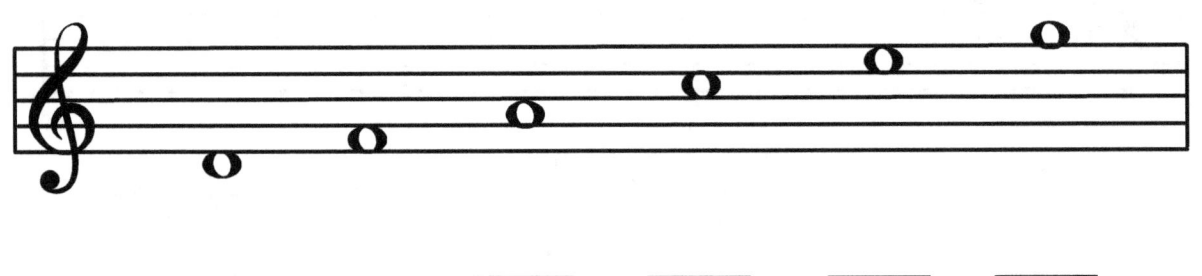

— — — — — — —

— — — — — — —

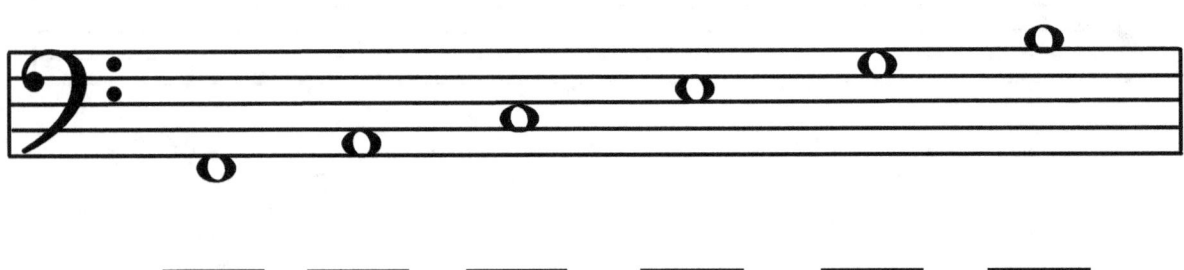

— — — — — — —

✏️ **Write the letter note before and after the note the little cat shows**

1. ____  ____  ____  A  ____  C

2. ____  A  ____  ____  ____  E

3. ____  ____  ____  A  ____  ____

4. ____  A  ____  ____  D  ____

5. ____  ____  ____  ____  A  ____

Easy Piano Learning for Kids | 43

**Match the note letter to the correct pitch**

A    B    C    D    E    F    G

**Name each note on the Treble Clef in the pineapple**

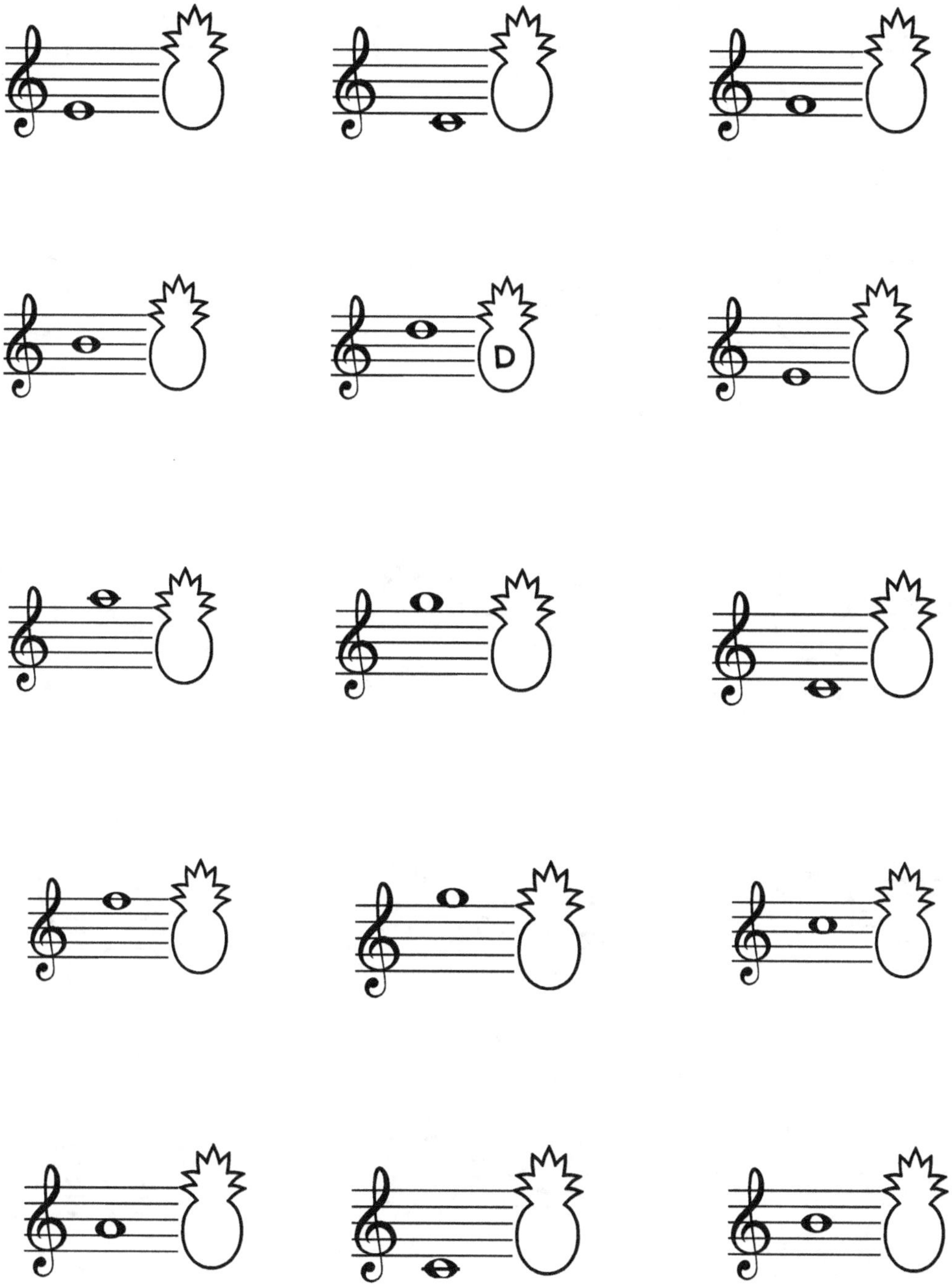

Easy Piano Learning for Kids | 45

✏️ **Name each note on the Bass Clef in the apple**

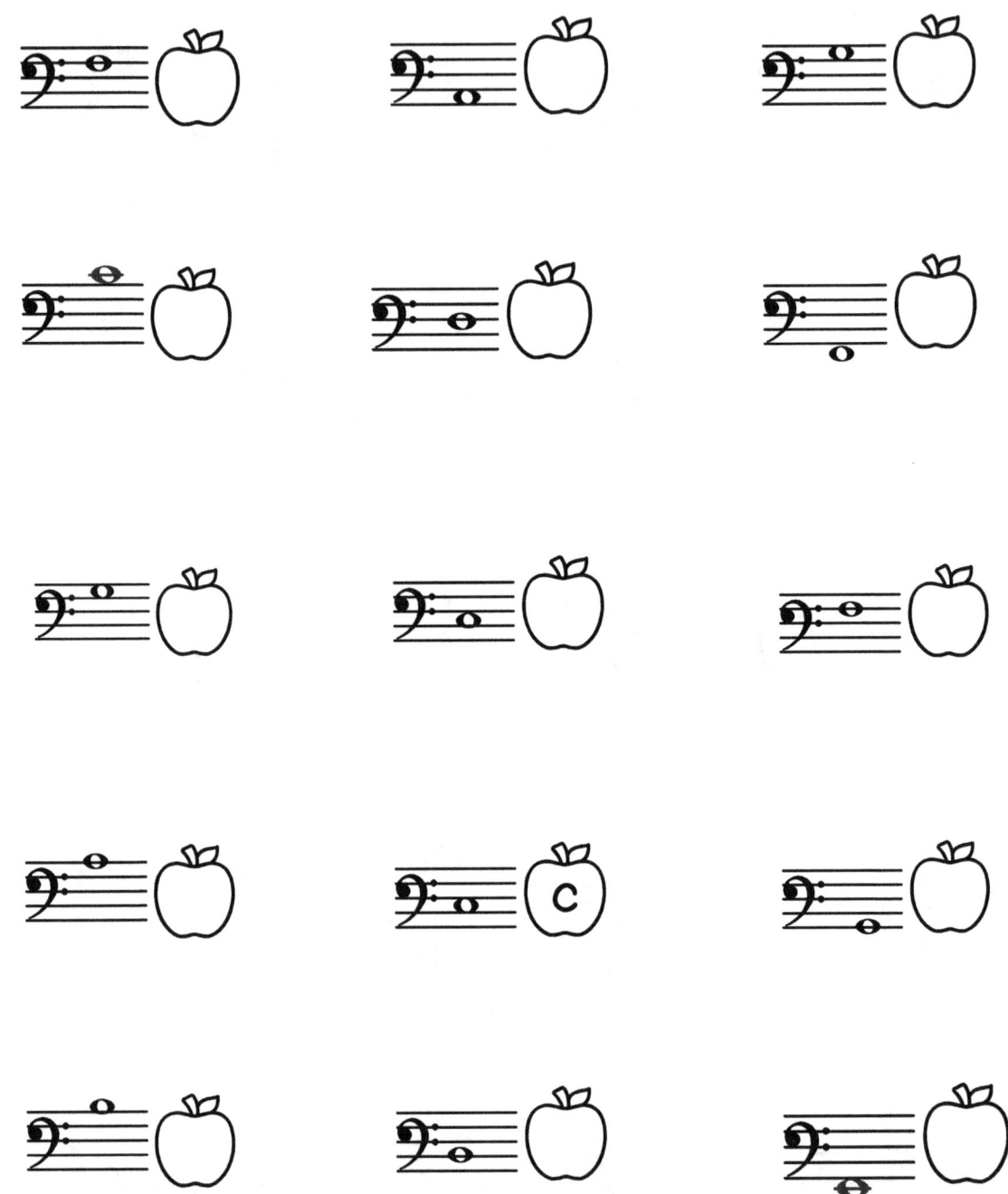

 **Match the note letter to the correct pitch**

**A    B    C    D    E    F    G**

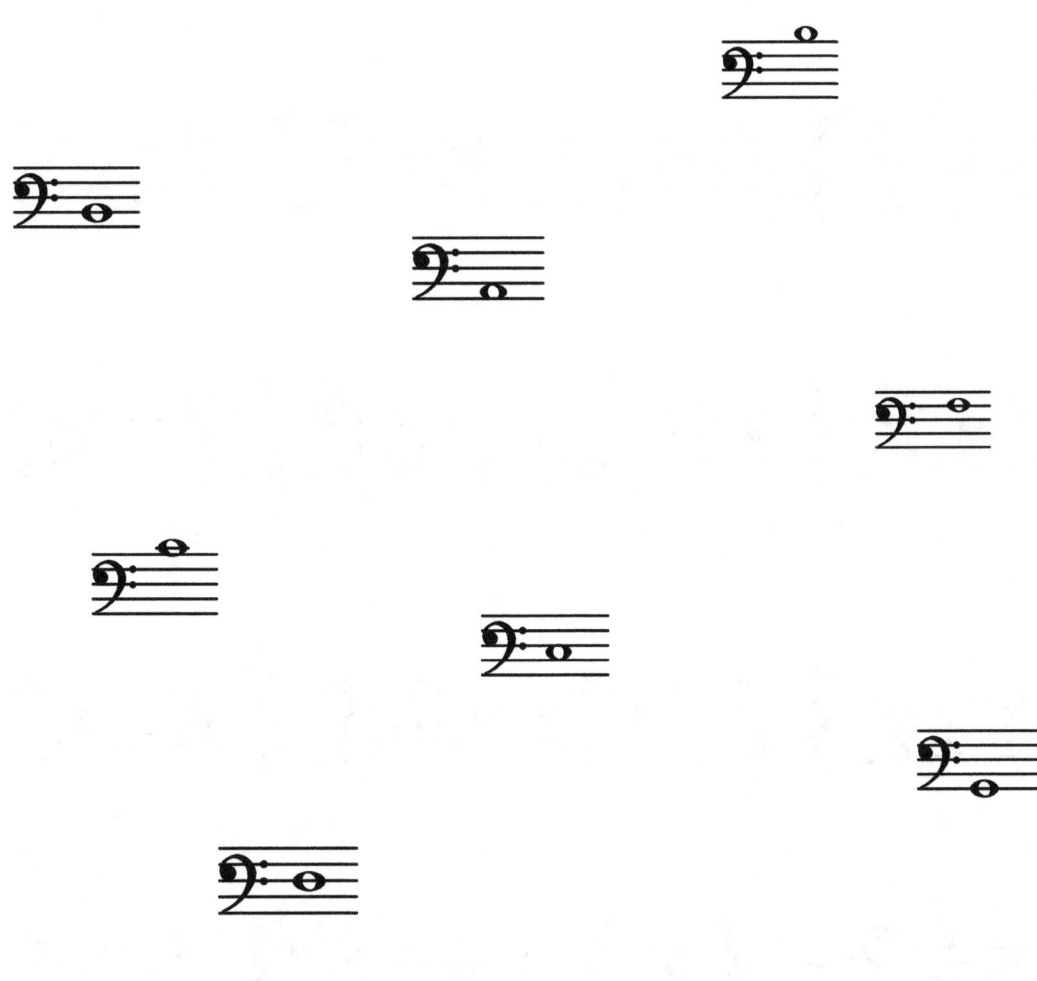

Name each note in the crab for the Bass Clef and in the fish for the Treble Clef

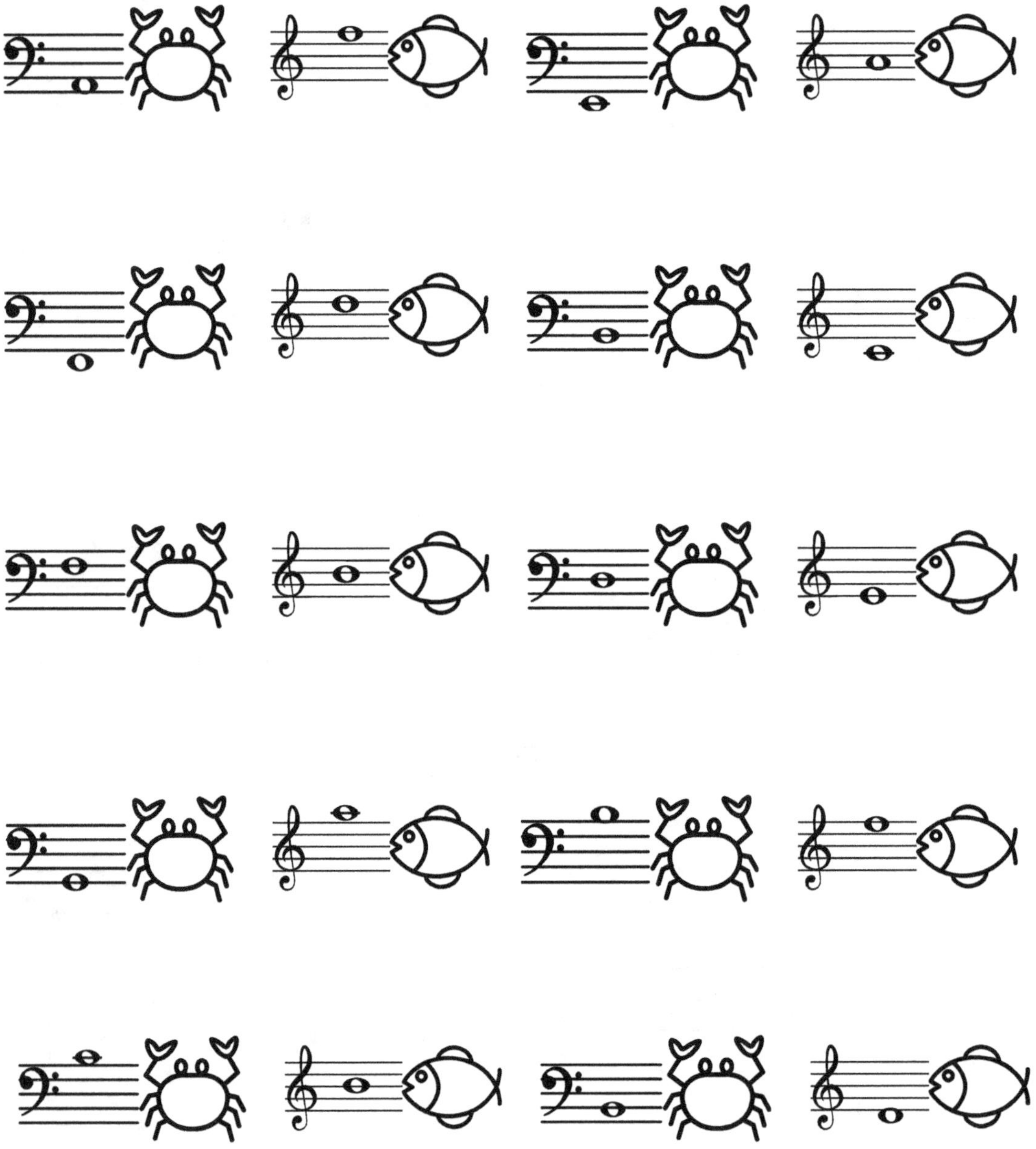

✏️ Write the note letter for each Bass and Treble Clef

Write a letter to Tooth Fairy with notes on Treble Clef

**Write the name of each note underneath**

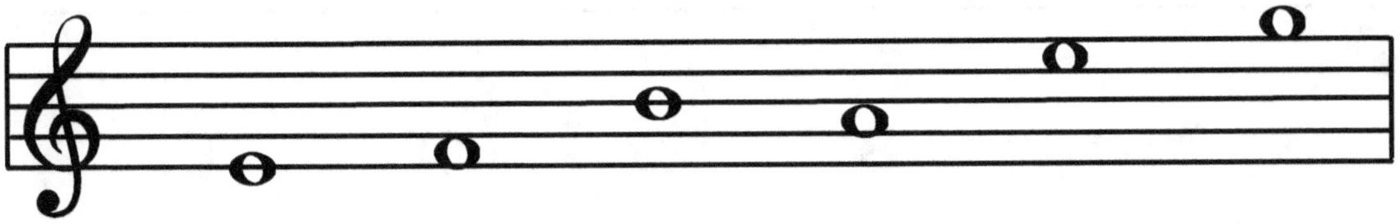

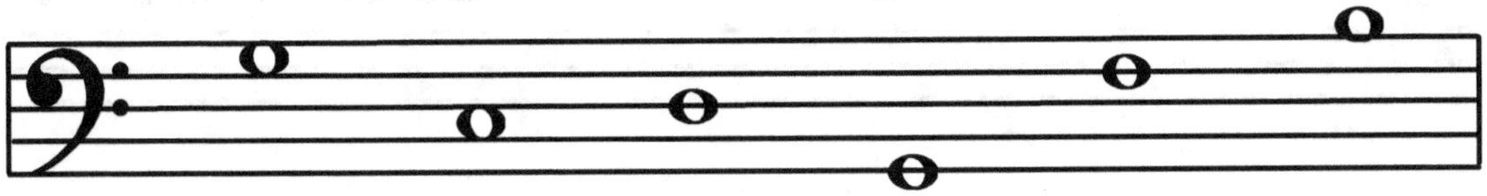

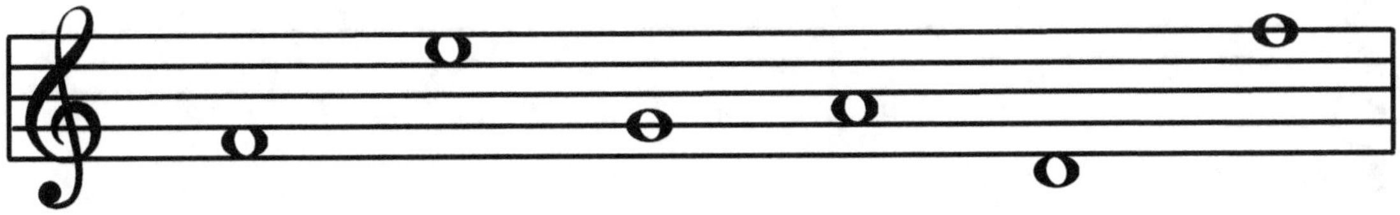

Write these notes on the staff

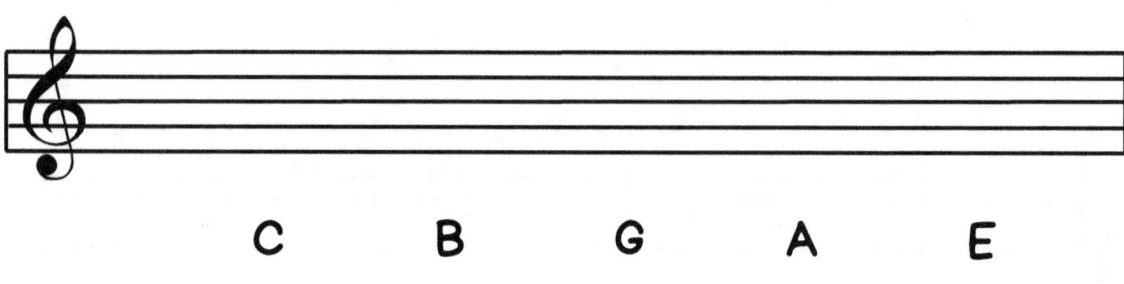

C　B　G　A　E

F　D　C　A　G

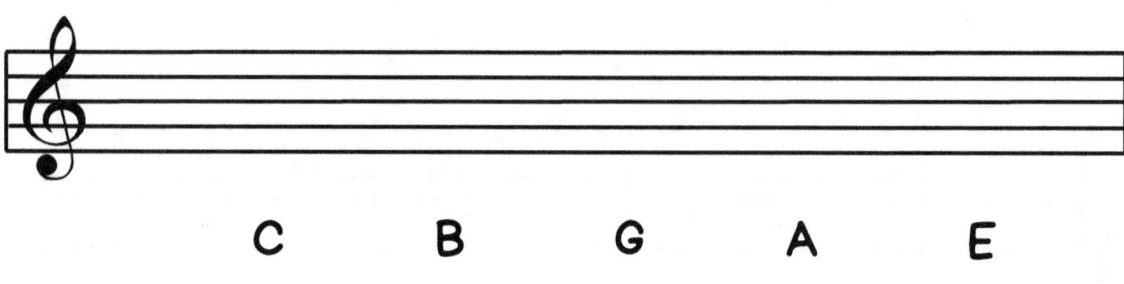

F　D　A　C　E

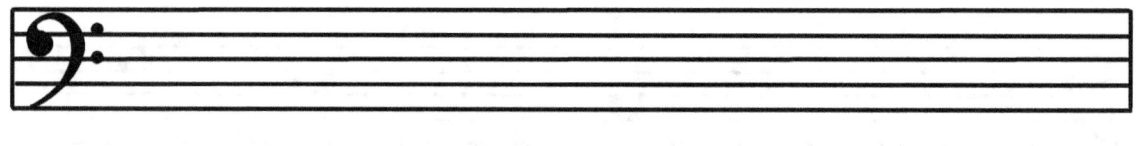

A　E　F　B　G

**Write the correct letter names inside the boxes to spell the words**

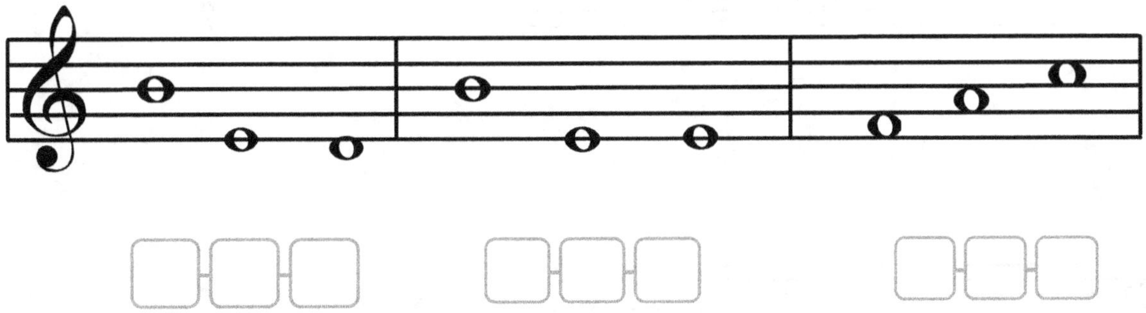

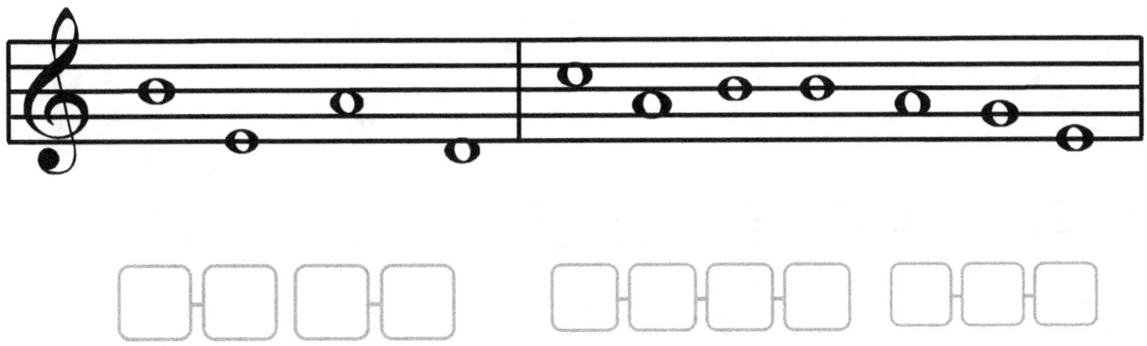

**Write the name of each shape as piano note on left and right hand**

FACE

EGG

BEE

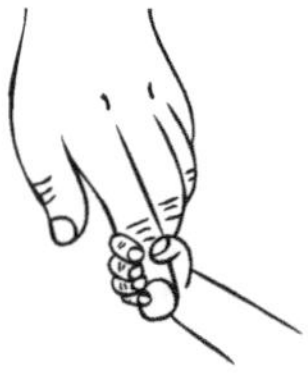

DAD

54 | Easy Piano Learning for Kids

**Write a letter to my pet with notes on Bass Clef:**

DEAr my p_t, I lov_ h_vin_ you _rond.

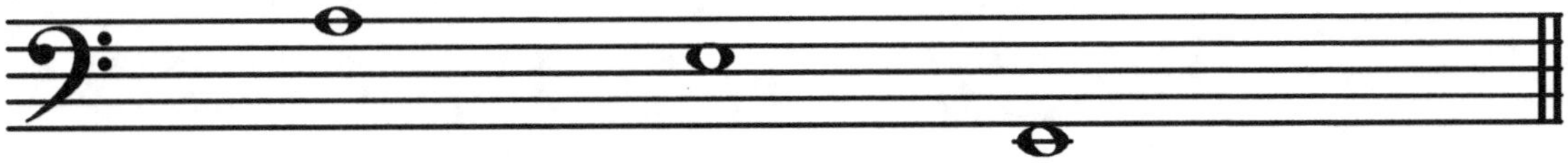

You -re my B_st fri_nd.

Tod_y w_s so mu_h fun pl_ying with you.

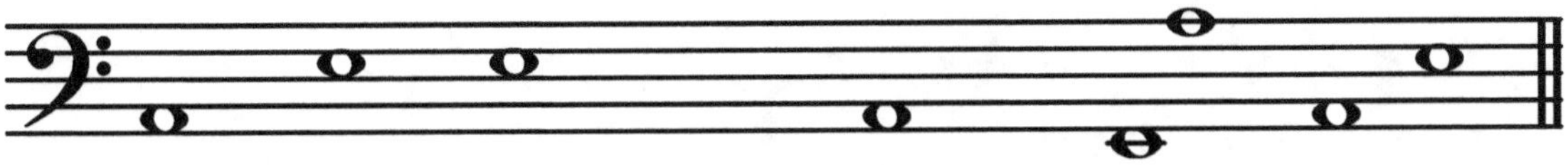

I'll m_ke sur_ to f_ed you your f_vorite tr_ _ts lAt_r.

I just w_nted to s_y how mu_h I lov_ you!    lov_,

# NOTES ON THE PIANO

# LESSON: 7 Basic Notes

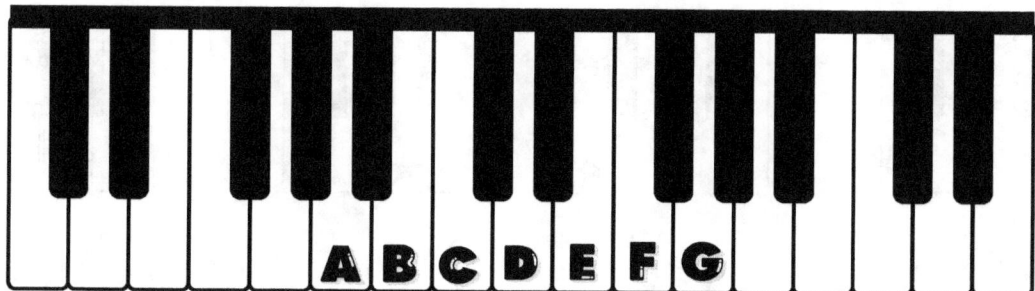

A Piano keyboard has a fun pattern with black and white keys.

The black keys come in group of two and three.

The white keys are in between and around the black keys.

The black keys help you find where the notes are, and each set of two and three black keys keeps repeating across the whole keyboard.

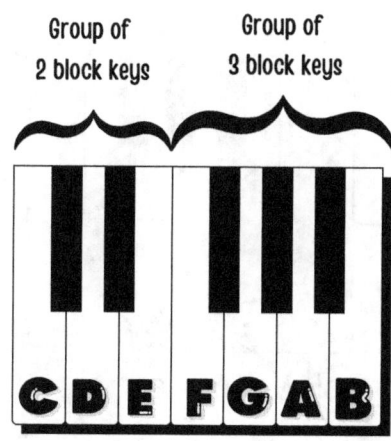

Easy Piano Learning for Kids

Circle the letter name for each key with star

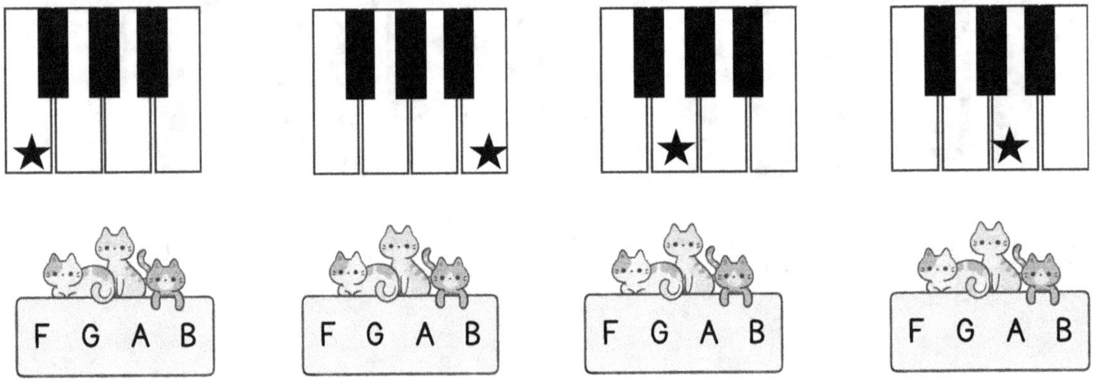

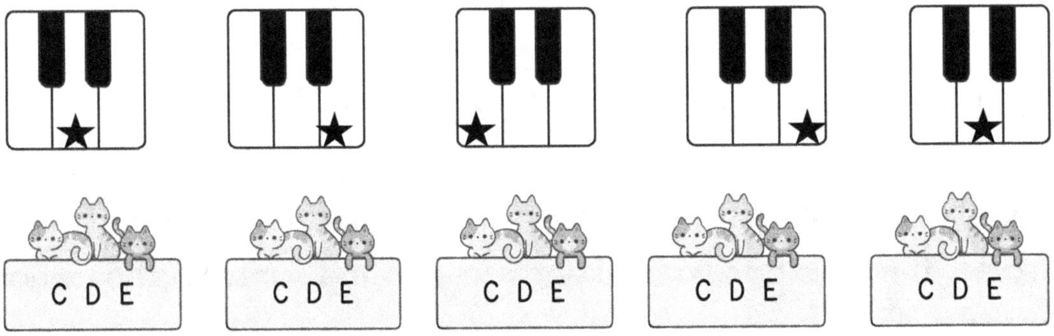

✏️ Circle the letter name for each key with moon

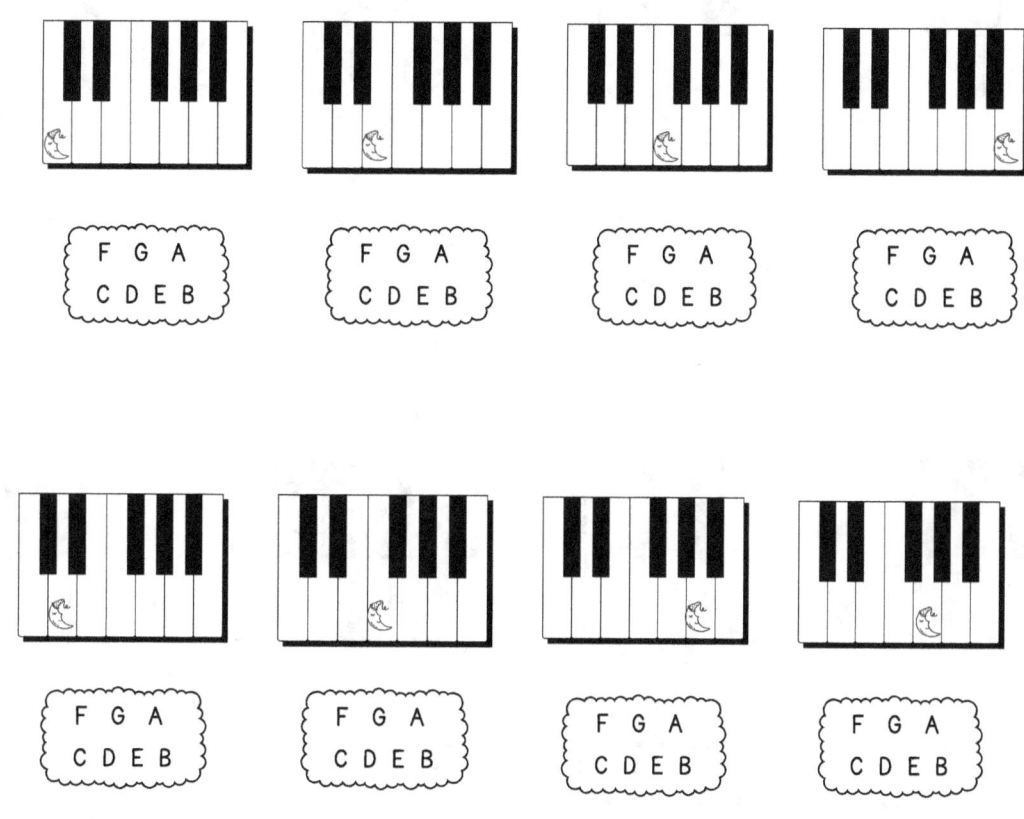

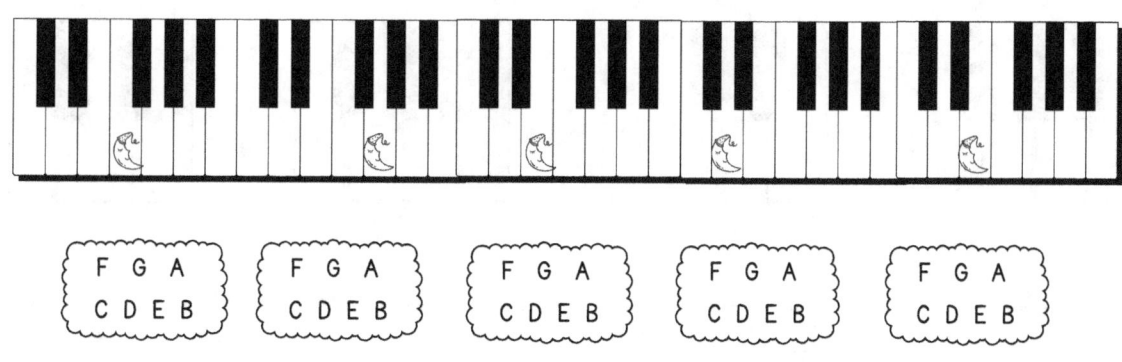

**Write the note name that each butterfly sits on for the piano keys**

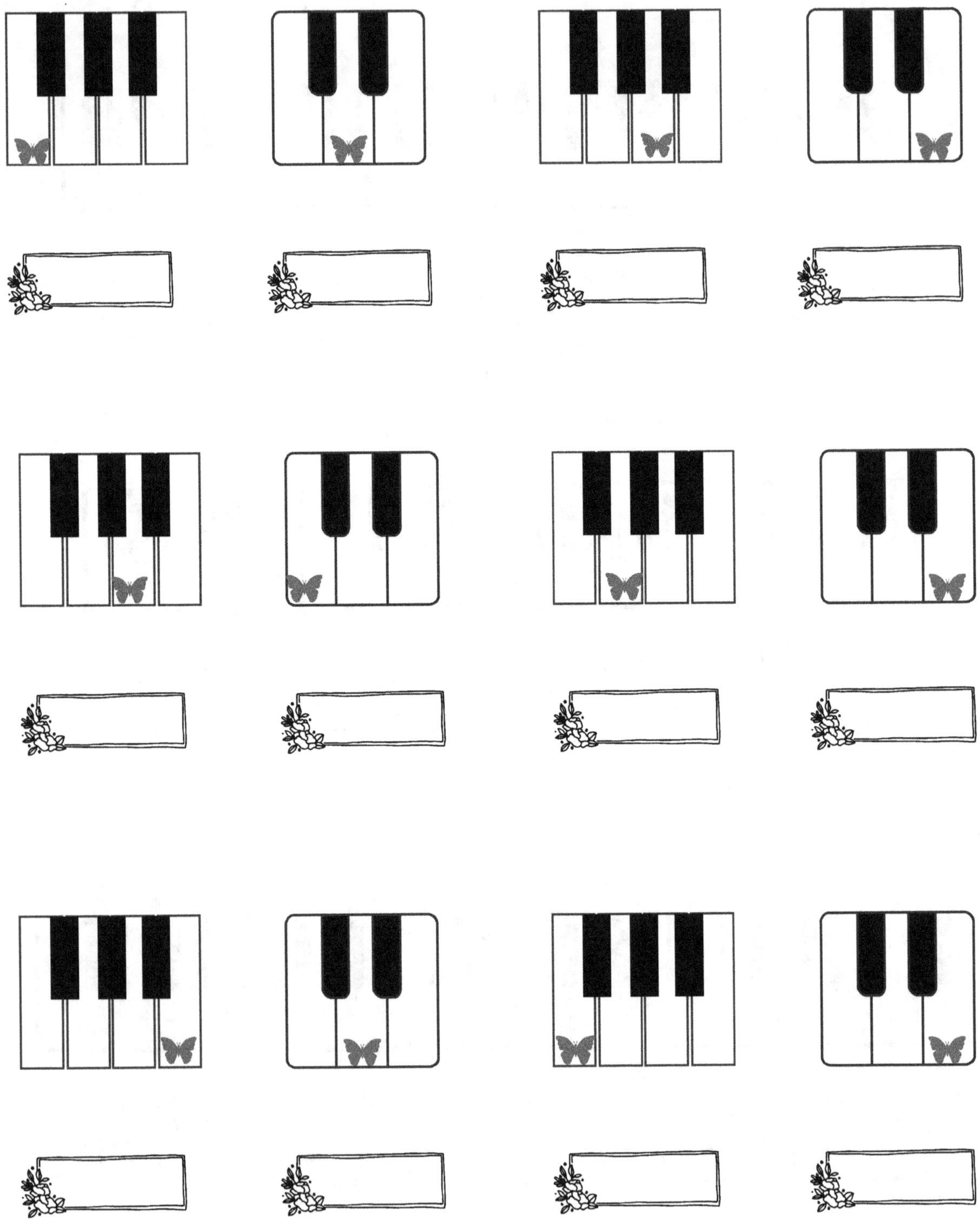

**Write the note that each snowflake shows on the piano keys**

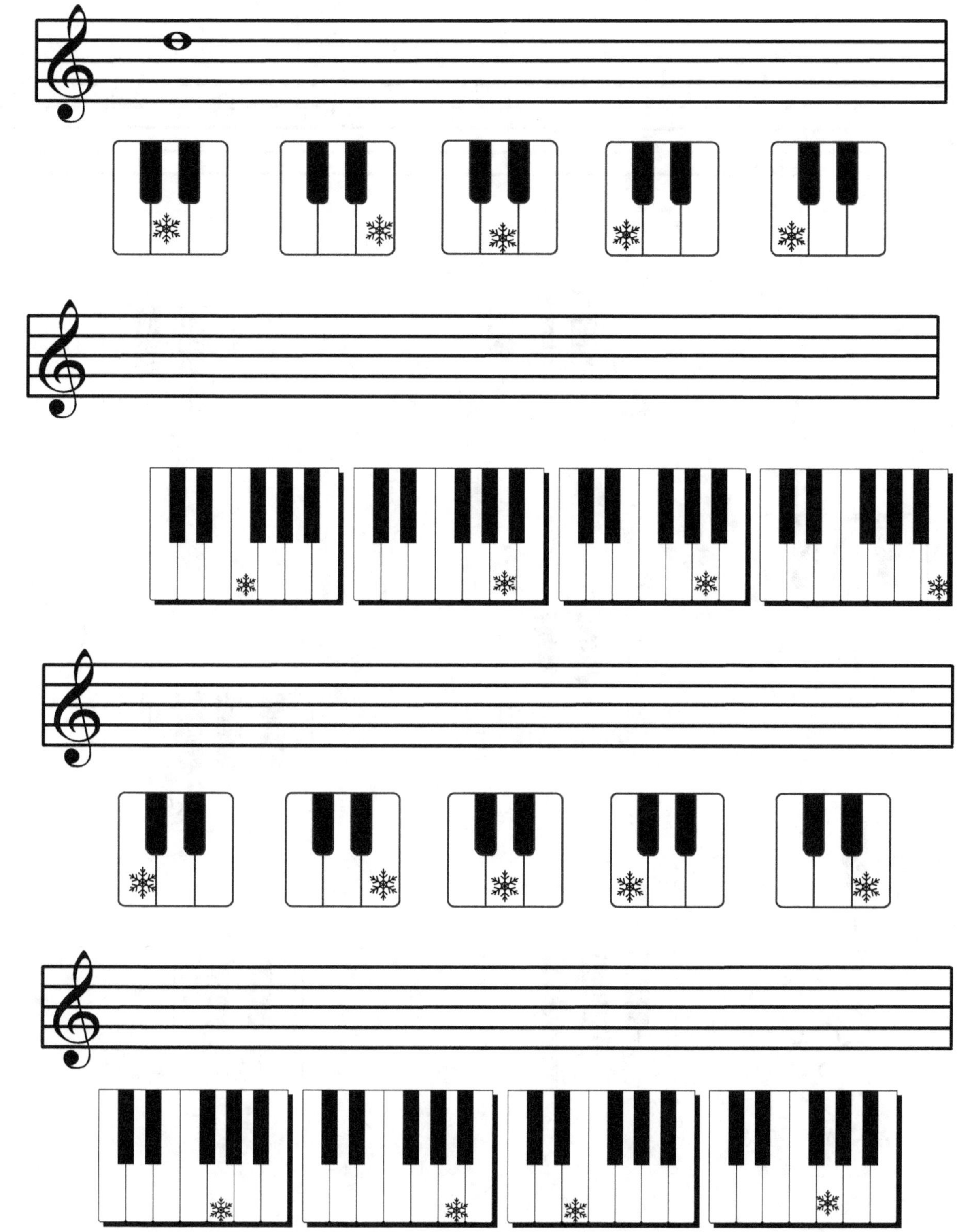

 **Locate each flower to the note in the bass staff**

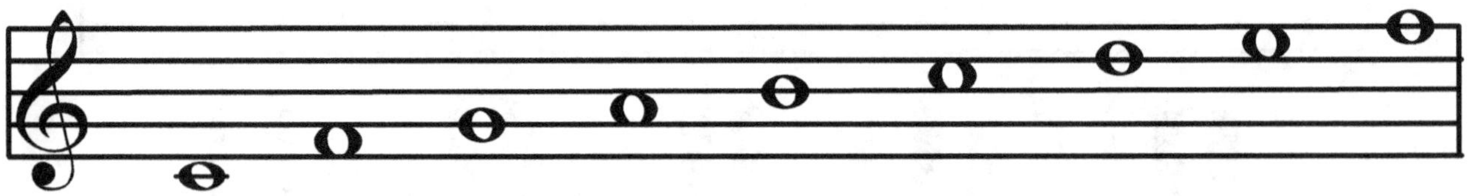

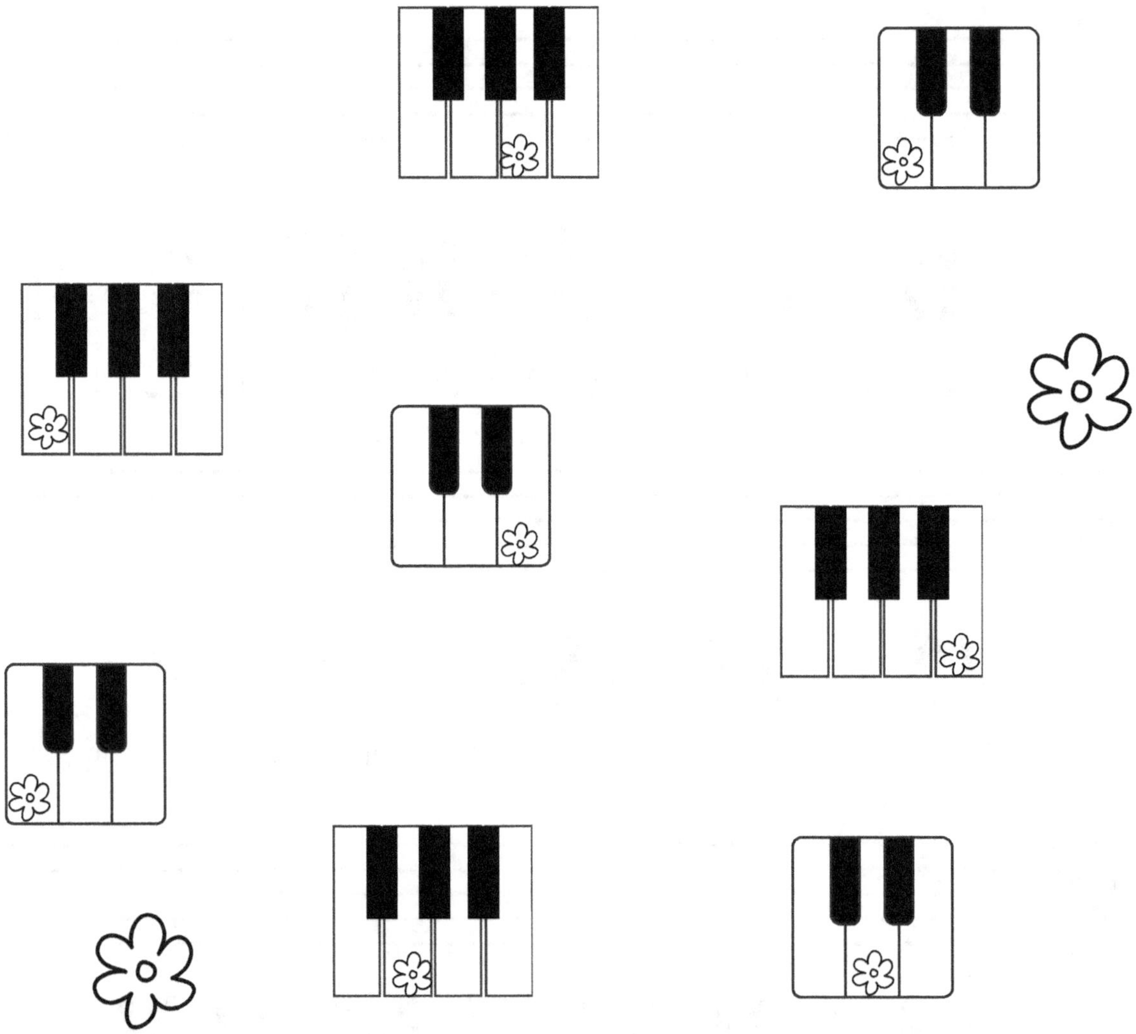

64 | Easy Piano Learning for Kids

 **Color by notes C, D, E, F, G, A, B on Treble Clef**

**Show relevant piano key for each letter in the star**

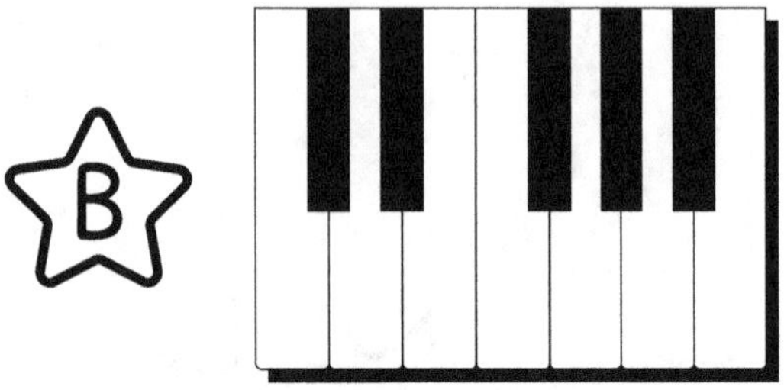

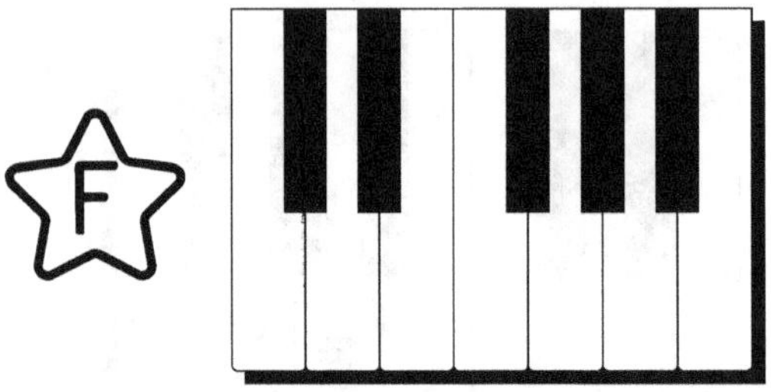

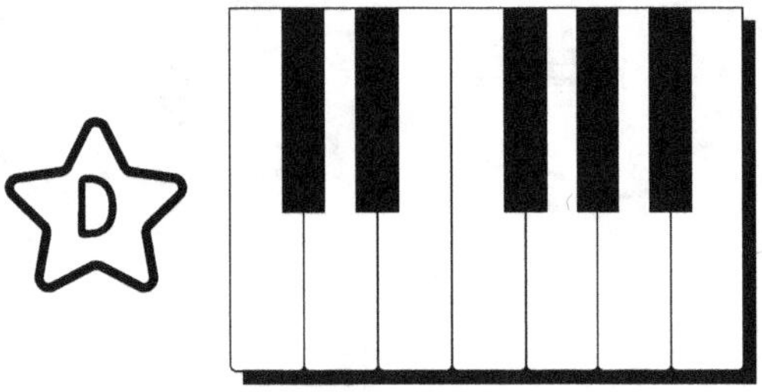

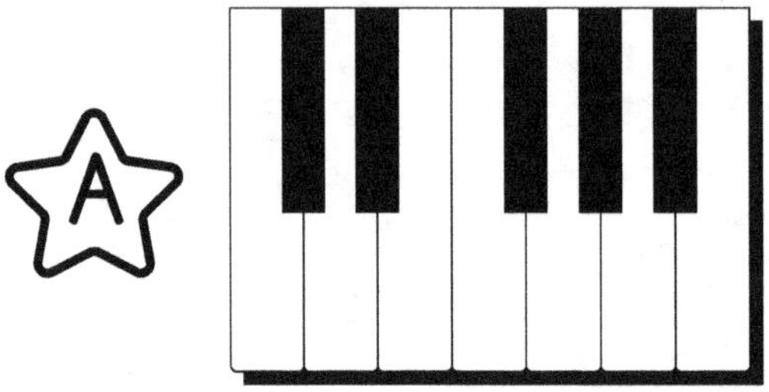

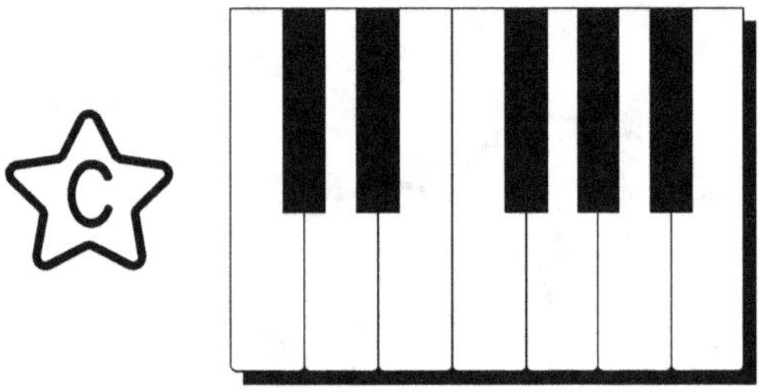

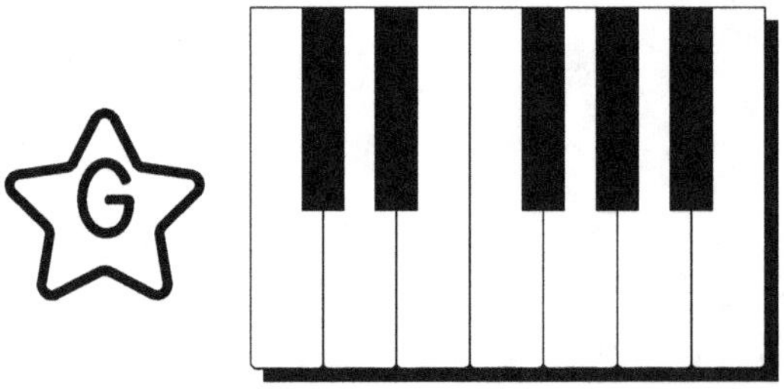

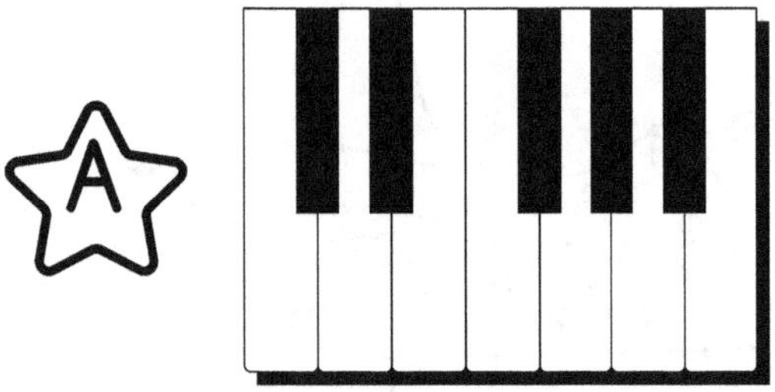

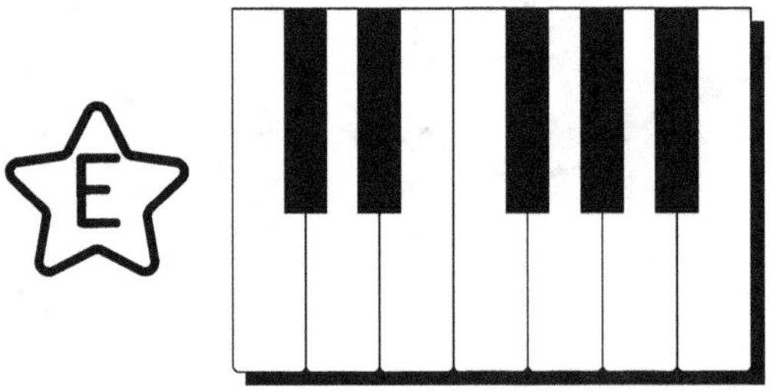

**Connect each group of letters to the relevant keys**

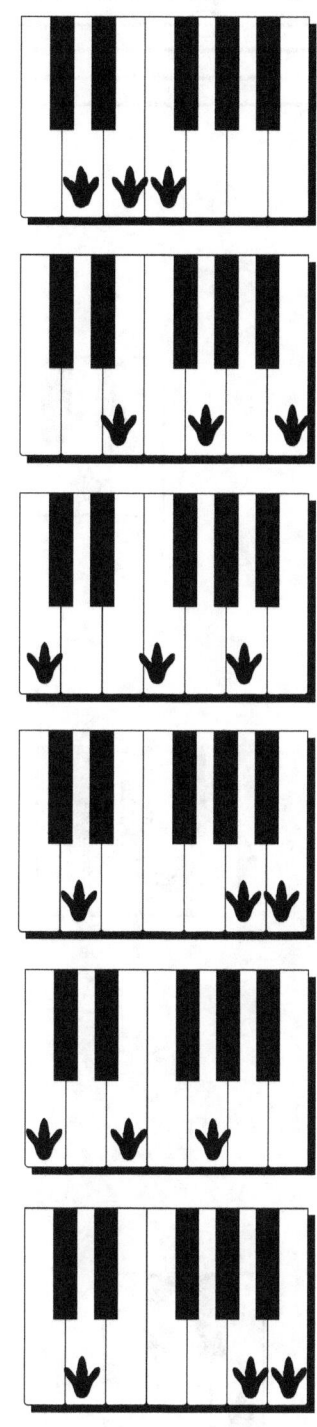

Easy Piano Learning for Kids | 67

Locate each star to the note in the bass staff

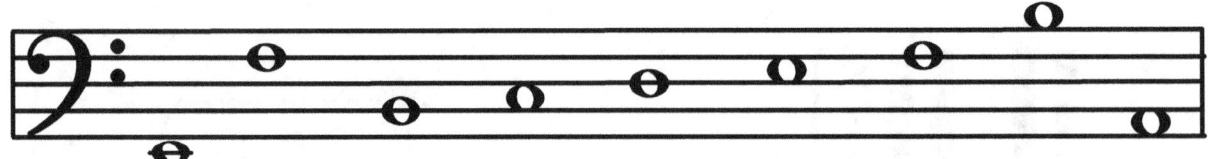

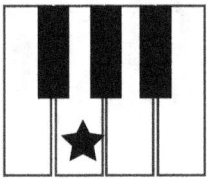

Locate each ladybug to the note in the bass staff

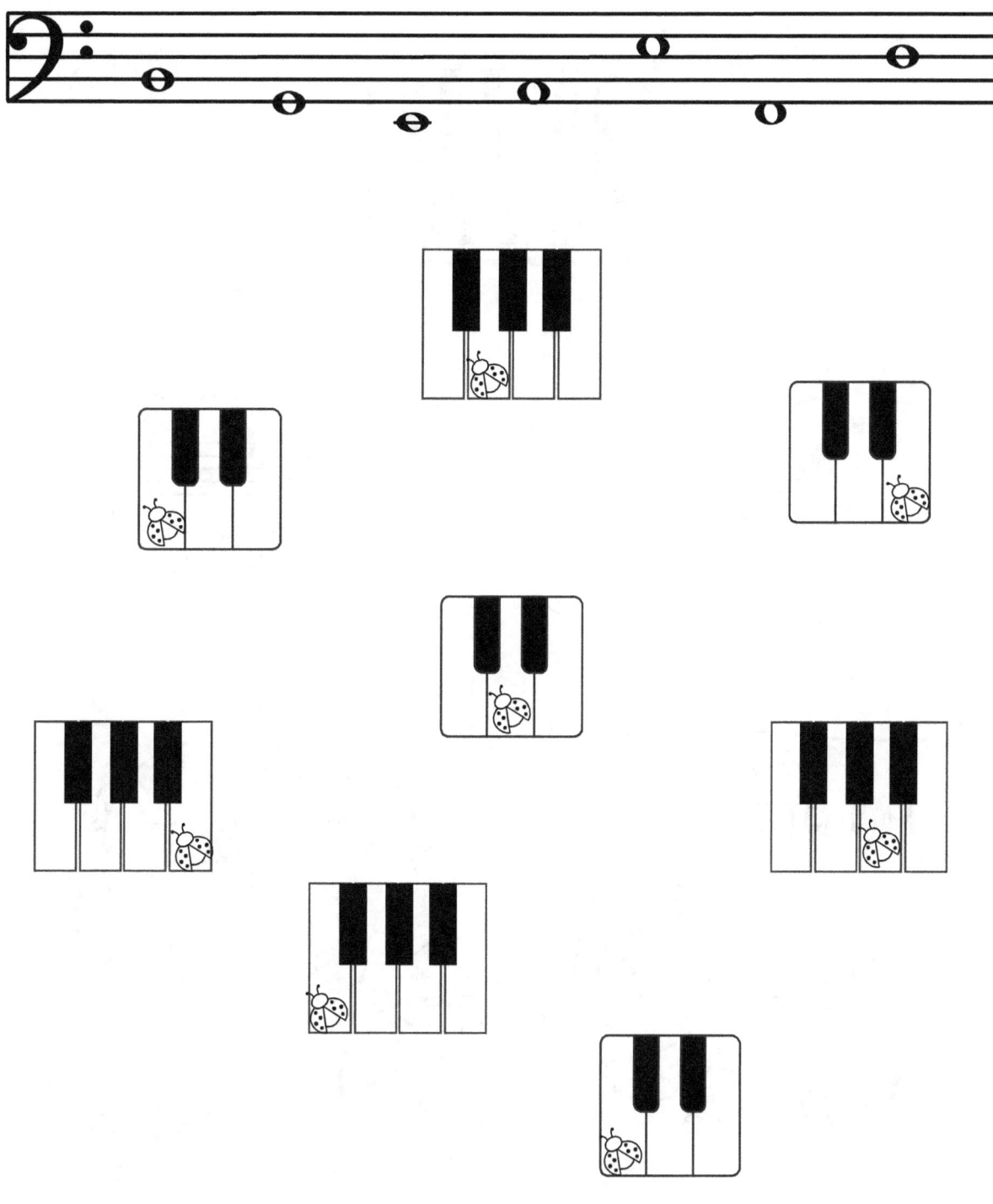

Easy Piano Learning for Kids | 69

 **Color by notes C, D, E, F, G, A, B on Bass Clef**

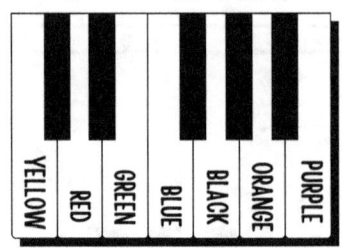

Name the piano keys and write the word in the cloud

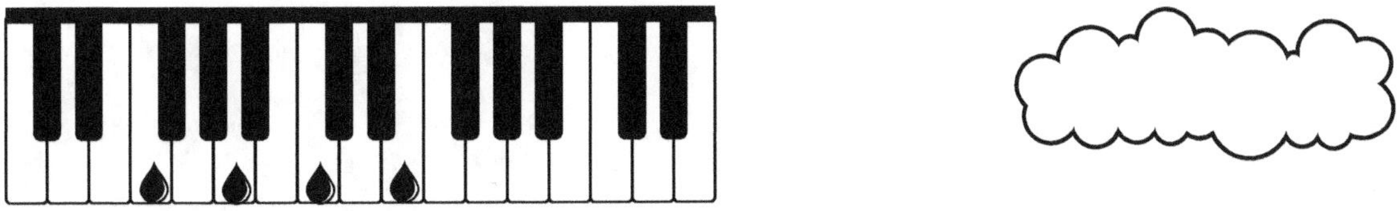

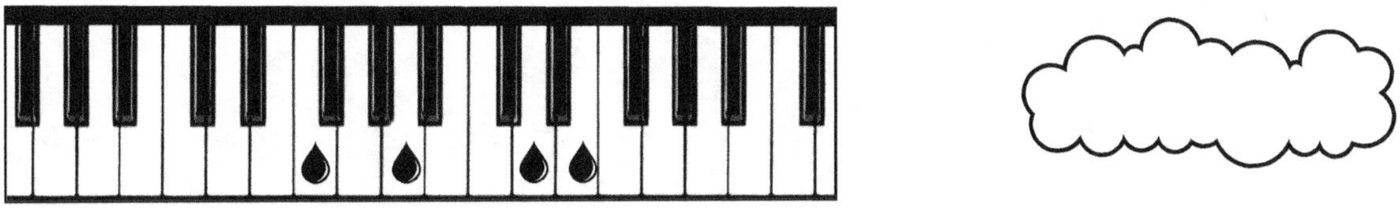

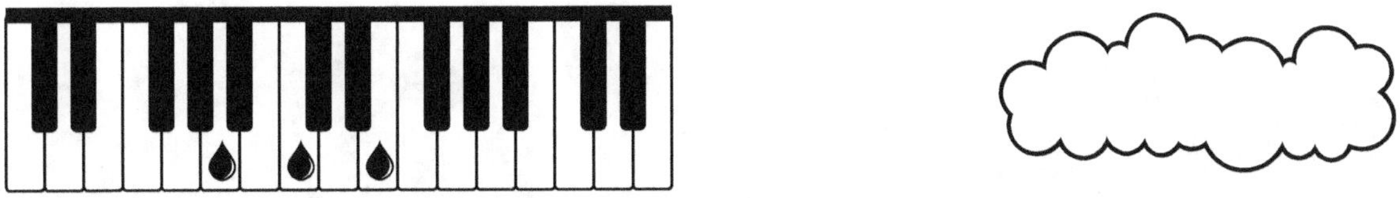

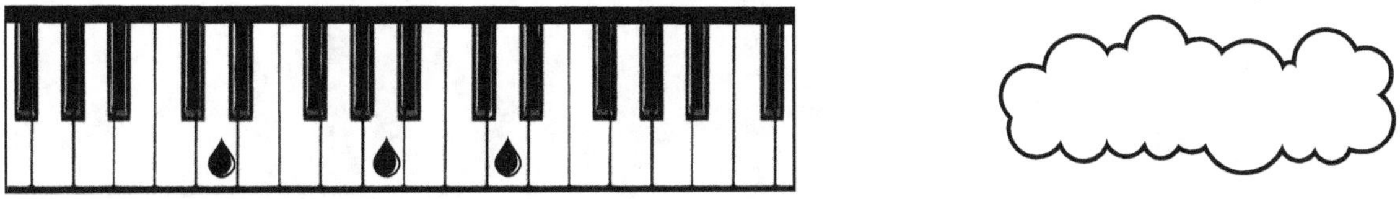

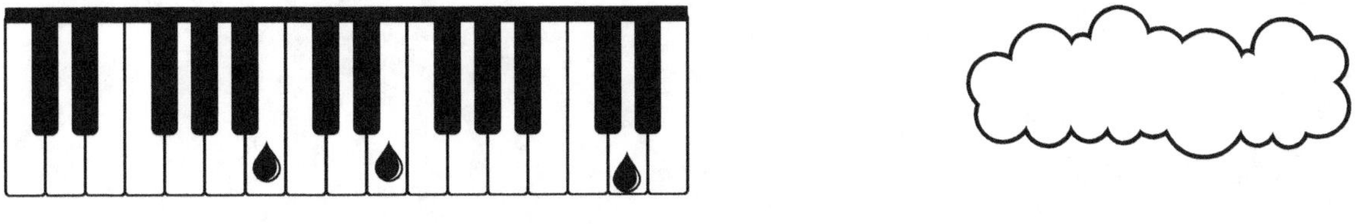

# NOTE VALUES AND RHYTHM

# LESSON: Rhythm notes and rests Counting

In this lesson, you are going to learn about how rhythm is represented in music notation.

Music rhythm explains that notes represent duration of sound, while rests represent duration of silence.

The value or number of beats of each note and rest determines the length of the sound or silence.

In the next lesson Mr. Maestro Mario will explain you the meaning of the values.

|  | NOTE | REST |
|---|---|---|
| WHOLE | 𝅝 | 𝄻 |
| HALF | 𝅗𝅥 | 𝄼 |
| QUARTER | ♩ | 𝄽 |
| EIGHT | ♪ | 𝄾 |

Easy Piano Learning for Kids | 75

Once upon a time in the bustling town of **Melodica**, there was a quaint little pizza shop called "**Notes 'n' Bites**".

The owner, **Maestro Mario**, had a unique way of selling his delicious pizzas - he sold them in bite-sized portions called **"bites"**.

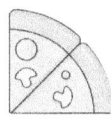

Each bite represented a fraction of the whole pizza. So, when a customer asked for **1 "bite"** they received a **Quarter** of the entire pizza.

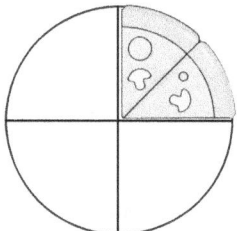

If someone wanted a bit more, say **Half** of the pizza, they'd request **2 "bites"**.

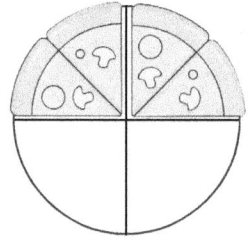

And for those with bigger appetites, a **Whole** pizza meant asking for **4 "bites"**.

Maestro Mario's pizza shop was not just about serving up tasty pies; it was also a place of learning.

One day, a group of curious kids wandered into the shop, eager to understand the mysterious world of music notes.

| PIZZA MENU | | |
|---|---|---|
| Whole pizza | 🍕 | 4 bites |
| Half pizza | 🍕 | 2 bites |
| Quarter pizza | 🍕 | 1 bite |
| Eighth pizza | 🍕 | 1/2 bite |

| MUSIC MENU | | |
|---|---|---|
| Whole note | 𝅝 | 4 beats |
| Half note | 𝅗𝅥 | 2 beats |
| Quarter note | ♩ | 1 beat |
| Eighth note | ♫ | 1/2 beat |

Easy Piano Learning for Kids | 77

A whole note is like a whole pizza - it has 4 beats value, just like 4 bites of pizza:

| | | |
|---|---|---|
| Whole pizza | 🍕 | 4 bites |
| Whole note | 𝅝 | 4 beats |

A half note, on the other hand, is like half of a pizza, receiving 2 beats value.

| | | |
|---|---|---|
| Half pizza | 🍕 | 2 bites |
| Half note | 𝅗𝅥 | 2 beats |

Then there's the quarter note, which is like a single bite of pizza - it gets just 1 beat value.

| | | |
|---|---|---|
| Quarter pizza | 🍕 | 1 bite |
| Quarter note | ♩ | 1 beat |

But wait, there's more!" Maestro Mario exclaimed, his eyes twinkling with excitement. "We have the eighth note, which is like half a bite of pizza - it receives only half a beat value!"

| | | |
|---|---|---|
| Eighth pizza | 🍕 | 1/2 bite |
| Eighth note | ♫ OR ♪ ♪ | 1/2 beat |

78 | Easy Piano Learning for Kids

The children's eyes widened with understanding as they compared the values of pizza bites with those of music notes.

"So, just as different bites make up a whole pizza", Maestro Mario concluded, "different notes come together to create beautiful music."

And from that day on, whenever the children played their instruments, they remembered the valuable lesson from Notes 'n' Bites – that every note, like every bite, had its own special place in the melody of life.

# LESSON: Rhythm notes Counting

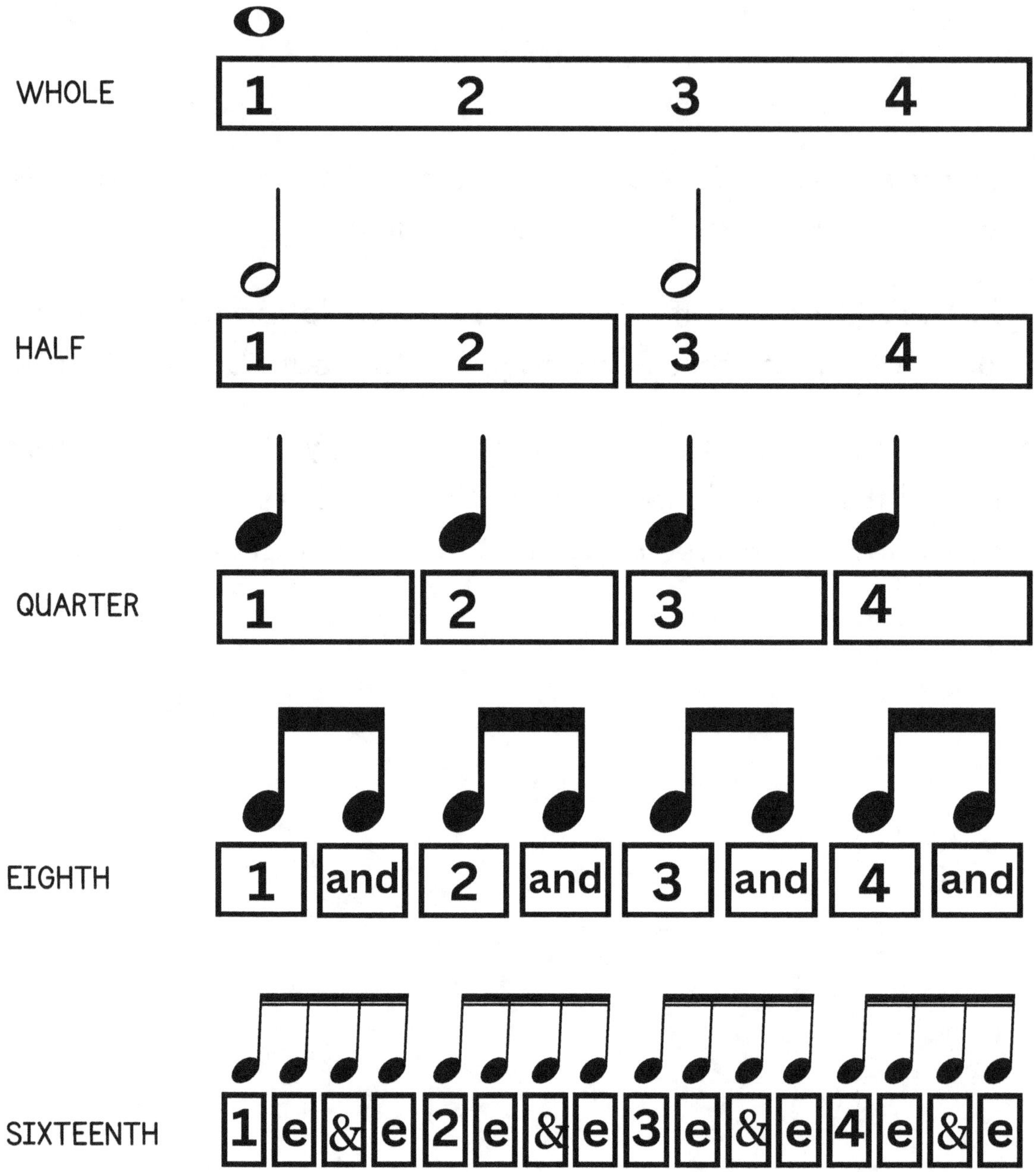

| WHOLE | 1 2 3 4 |

| HALF | 1 2 | 3 4 |

| QUARTER | 1 | 2 | 3 | 4 |

| EIGHTH | 1 and 2 and 3 and 4 and |

| SIXTEENTH | 1 e & e 2 e & e 3 e & e 4 e & e |

**& = and**

**Connect each note to its name**

**Connect the values in each moon to the relevant note and rest in the stars**

**Draw a line to connect each note to its number of counts**

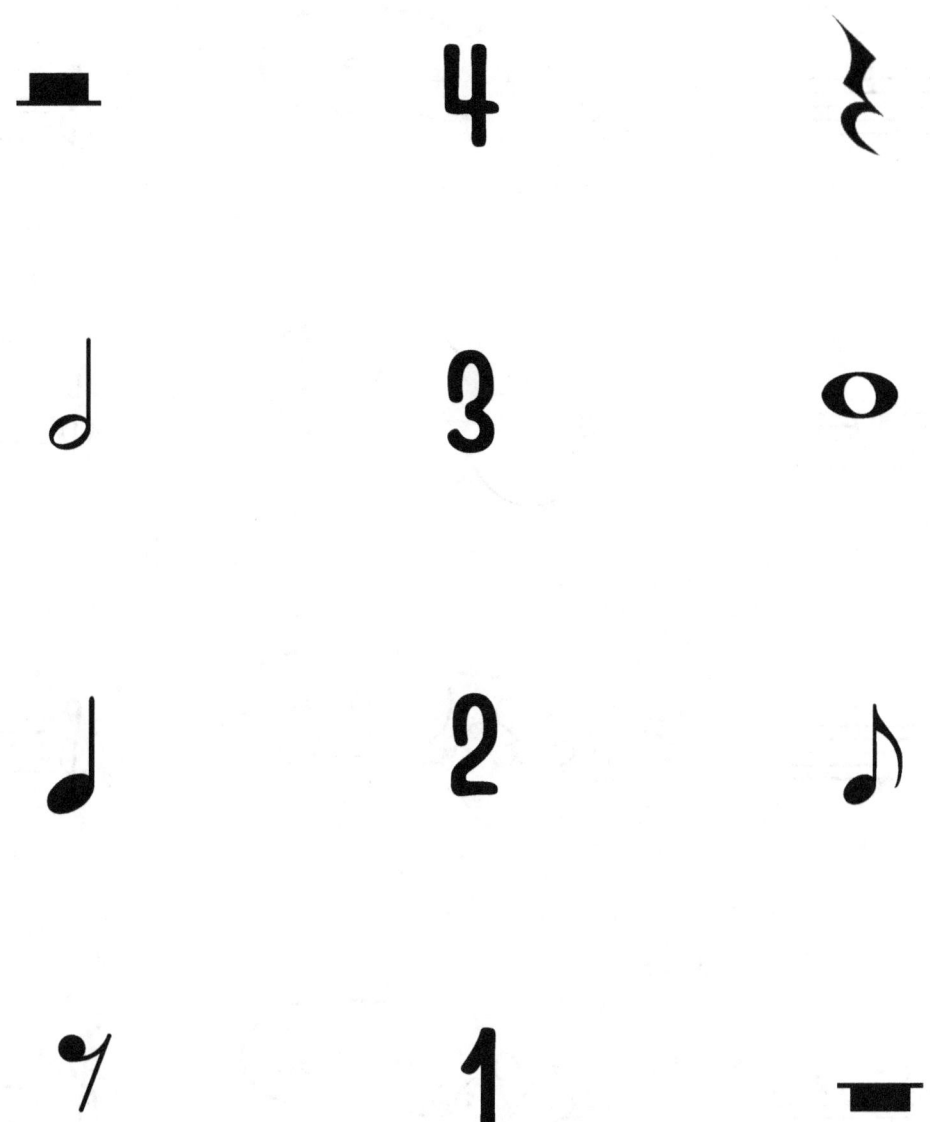

**Connect each note and rest to the value that the bird calls**

🖉 Draw the notes or rests in each ornament as named on the line below each one

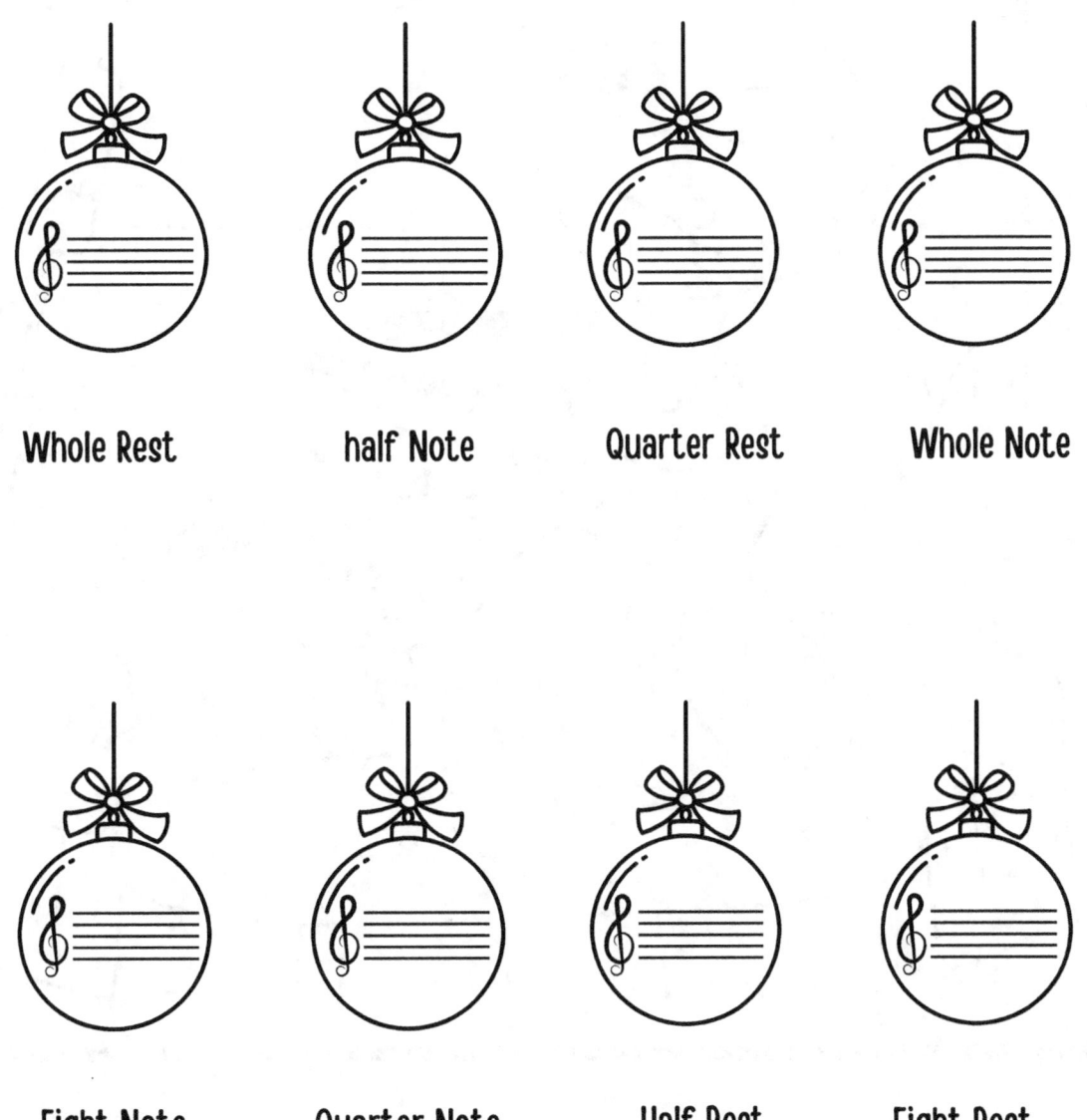

**Whole Rest**  **half Note**  **Quarter Rest**  **Whole Note**

**Eight Note**  **Quarter Note**  **Half Rest**  **Eight Rest**

 **Color Time**

| | | | |
|---|---|---|---|
| 1 beat | Blue | 2 beats | Dark Green |
| half rest | Red | quarter beat | Light Green |
| half beat | Yellow | 4 beats | Brown |

 **Color the ice creams based on the notes or rests values**

This is half rest and has value of 2, so color 2 ice creams

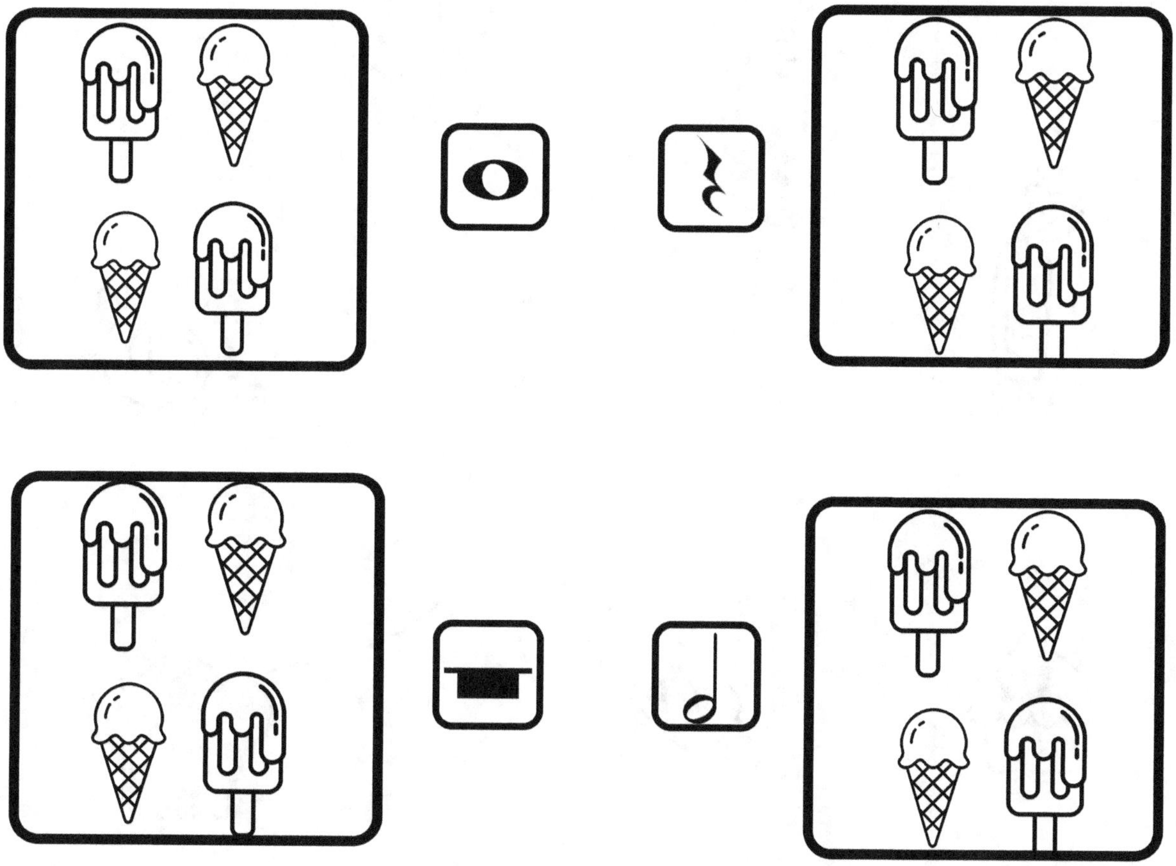

Match the candies with the cookies that have the same total number of beats and color them the same color

**Notes or Rests**

Write the name of the note or rest on the line below each cloud

_____   _____   _____   _____

_____   _____   _____   _____

 Write how many beats the shown notes and rests in each cherry get

 **Add the note values**

𝅝 + ♩ = _____ BEATS

♩ + 𝅝 = _____ BEATS

♩ + ♩ = _____ BEATS

𝅝 + ♩ = _____ BEATS

♩ + ♩ = _____ BEATS

# Add the note values

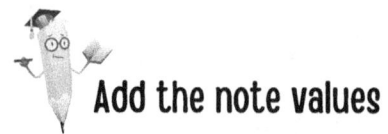

■ + ♩ = ____ BEATS

♩ + 𝄽 = ____ BEATS

𝅗𝅥 + ■ = ____ BEATS

𝄽 + ♩ = ____ BEATS

# Add the note values

 Color Time

| Whole Note | Yellow | Whole Rest | Light Blue | Half Note | Red |
| Half Rest | Green | Quarter Note | Purple | Quarter Rest | Pink |
| Eight note | Dark Blue | Eight Rest | Black | | |

**Hey Parents,**

If your kids are enjoying "Easy Piano Learning for Kids", I'd love to hear about it! Please scan the QR code below and share your honest thoughts on Amazon. Your review can help other parents and teachers decide if this book is a good fit for their young learners. Thanks a bunch!

| USA | UK | CANADA |
|---|---|---|
|  |  |  |

*Cheers,*
*Clara Forte*

www.ingramcontent.com/pod-product-compliance
Lightning Source LLC
Chambersburg PA
CBHW082211070526
44585CB00020B/2374